D1645998

STAR TREK
THE NEXT GENERATION®
GHOSTS

BR10(

Bristol Libraries

1802444054

STAR TREK
THE NEXT GENERATION®
GHOSTS

Written by **ZANDER CANNON**

Art by **JAVIER ARANDA**

Inks by **GERMAN TORRES-RUIZ**
and **MARC RUEDA**

Colors by **John Hunt**

Letters by **Robbie Robbins**
and **Neil Uyetake**

Original Series Edits by **Scott Dunbier**

Collection Edits by **Justin Eisinger**

Cover by **Joe Corroney**

Collection Design by **Gilberto Lazcano**

BRISTOL CITY LIBRARIES	
AN1802444054	
PE	23-Sep-2010
JF	£14.99

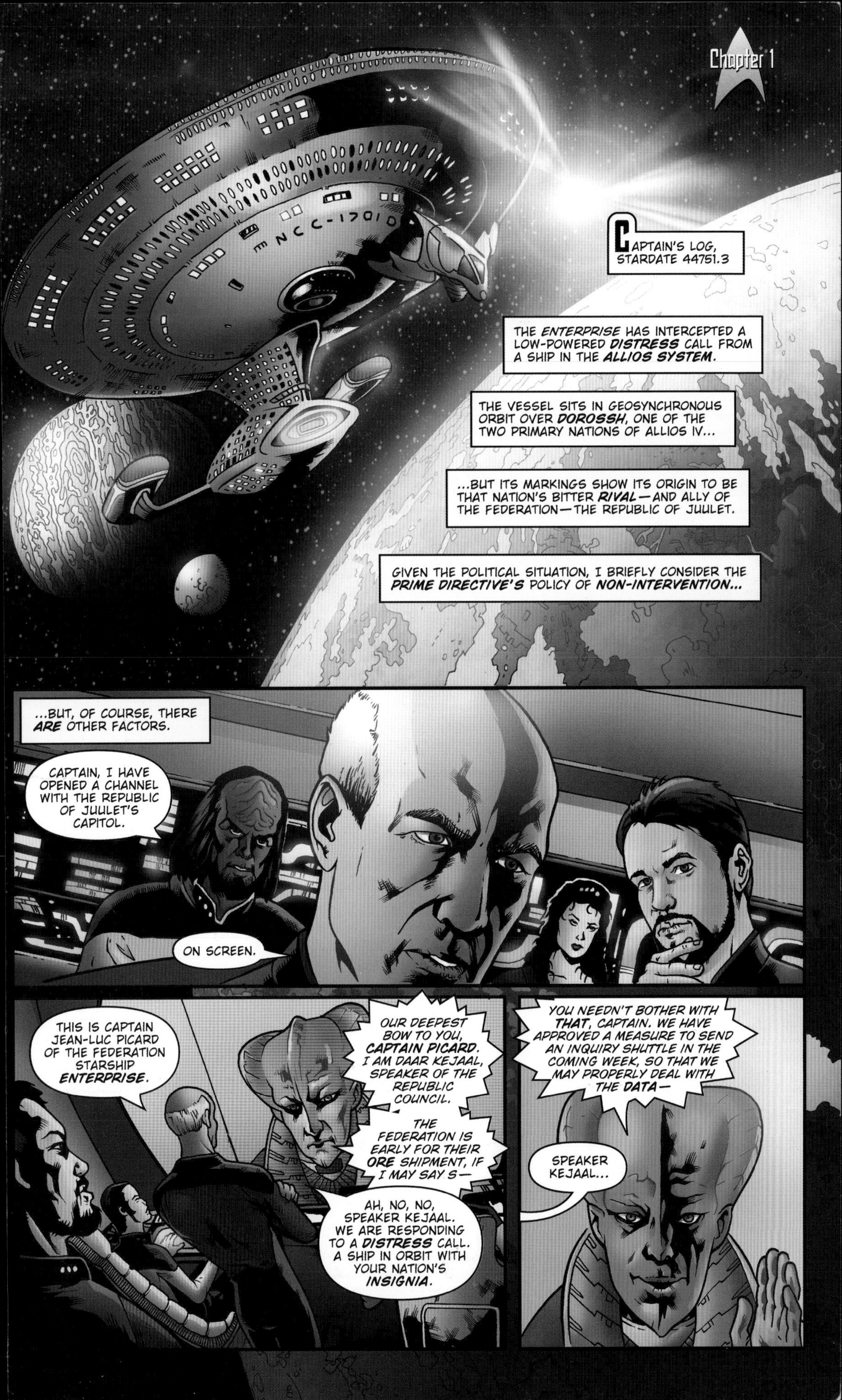
Chapter 1
CAPTAIN'S LOG, STARDATE 44751.3
THE ENTERPRISE HAS INTERCEPTED A LOW-POWERED DISTRESS CALL FROM A SHIP IN THE ALLIOS SYSTEM.
THE VESSEL SITS IN GEOSYNCHRONOUS ORBIT OVER DOROSSH, ONE OF THE TWO PRIMARY NATIONS OF ALLIOS IV...
...BUT ITS MARKINGS SHOW ITS ORIGIN TO BE THAT NATION'S BITTER RIVAL—AND ALLY OF THE FEDERATION—THE REPUBLIC OF JUULET.
GIVEN THE POLITICAL SITUATION, I BRIEFLY CONSIDER THE PRIME DIRECTIVE'S POLICY OF NON-INTERVENTION...
...BUT, OF COURSE, THERE ARE OTHER FACTORS.
CAPTAIN, I HAVE OPENED A CHANNEL WITH THE REPUBLIC OF JUULET'S CAPITOL.
ON SCREEN.
THIS IS CAPTAIN JEAN-LUC PICARD OF THE FEDERATION STARSHIP ENTERPRISE.
OUR DEEPEST BOW TO YOU, CAPTAIN PICARD. I AM DAAR KEJAAL, SPEAKER OF THE REPUBLIC COUNCIL.
THE FEDERATION IS EARLY FOR THEIR ORE SHIPMENT, IF I MAY SAY S—
AH, NO, NO, SPEAKER KEJAAL. WE ARE RESPONDING TO A DISTRESS CALL. A SHIP IN ORBIT WITH YOUR NATION'S INSIGNIA.
YOU NEEDN'T BOTHER WITH THAT, CAPTAIN. WE HAVE APPROVED A MEASURE TO SEND AN INQUIRY SHUTTLE IN THE COMING WEEK, SO THAT WE MAY PROPERLY DEAL WITH THE DATA—
SPEAKER KEJAAL...

...WITH ALL DUE **RESPECT**, BOTH THE DISTRESS BEACON AND OUR SENSORS INDICATE A LIFE READING ABOARD THE VESSEL.

THE DISTRESS CALL HAS **ALREADY** BEEN SOUNDING FOR 31 HOURS, ALMOST A **FULL DAY** FOR YOU.

--AHEM-- WHAT COMMANDER RIKER MEANS IS... IT'S NO **TROUBLE**, SPEAKER KEJAAL. BUT WE FEEL THAT TIME IS OF THE **ESSENCE**.

OUR CHIEF CONCERN IS TO FIND THE **SURVIVOR** AND ASSURE YOU HE OR SHE IS **SAFE**.

YOUR INQUIRY SHUTTLE MAY THEN TAKE ALL THE TIME IT NEEDS TO INSPECT THE VESSEL AND THE DATA.

HMM. YES, VERY WELL, CAPTAIN PICARD. OUR SHUTTLE WILL HANDLE THE DATA RETRIEVAL. BUT YOUR PEOPLE REALLY NEED NOT BOTHER WITH SUCH A TRIFLE.

EXCELLENT. THEN WE'LL—

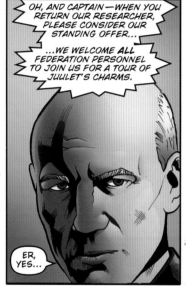

OH, AND CAPTAIN—WHEN YOU RETURN OUR RESEARCHER, PLEASE CONSIDER OUR STANDING OFFER...

...WE WELCOME **ALL** FEDERATION PERSONNEL TO JOIN US FOR A TOUR OF JUULET'S CHARMS.

ER, YES...

...A GENEROUS OFFER, SPEAKER KEJAAL. PERHAPS OUR SCHEDULE WILL ALLOW IT.

THANK YOU, CAPTAIN. WE LOOK FORWARD TO SEEING YOU.

NUMBER ONE, ASSEMBLE AN AWAY TEAM.

SIR.

AND, COMMANDER DATA—

—WHAT IS THE STATUS OF ALLIOS IV'S APPLICATION TO THE FEDERATION?

THEY HAVE BEEN WAIT-LISTED FOR ELEVEN YEARS, CAPTAIN.

THE REASON GIVEN IS ONGOING CIVIL WAR.

A WAR THAT THE REPUBLIC OF JUULET DENIES **EXISTS**.

THEY CLAIM TO SPEAK FOR THE ENTIRE PLANET, SIR...

IT'S *LUDICROUS.*

WHAT IS, WILL?

THAT IT SEEMS THEIR LEADER WOULD RISK LETTING THIS SURVIVOR DIE FOR A LITTLE POLITICAL *CAPITAL.*

TO PROVE THEY'RE READY FOR THE FEDERATION?

MAYBE.

ALL RIGHT, MR. LAFORGE, FIND THE SOURCE OF THE DISTRESS BEACON, CALL UP THE CREW MANIFEST, AND SEE IF YOU CAN FIGURE OUT WHAT *HAPPENED* HERE.

AYE, SIR.

HMM... DOESN'T LOOK LIKE THE SHIP IS EVEN *DAMAGED...*

DR. CRUSHER, COME WITH *ME.*

THE SURVIVOR IS *OUR* FIRST PRIORITY...

...EVEN IF IT ISN'T HIS *COUNTRYMEN'S.*

LET'S GRAB HIM AND GET OUT.

WITH THEIR RELUCTANCE TO LET US HELP, MY GUESS IS...

⊰GASP!⊱

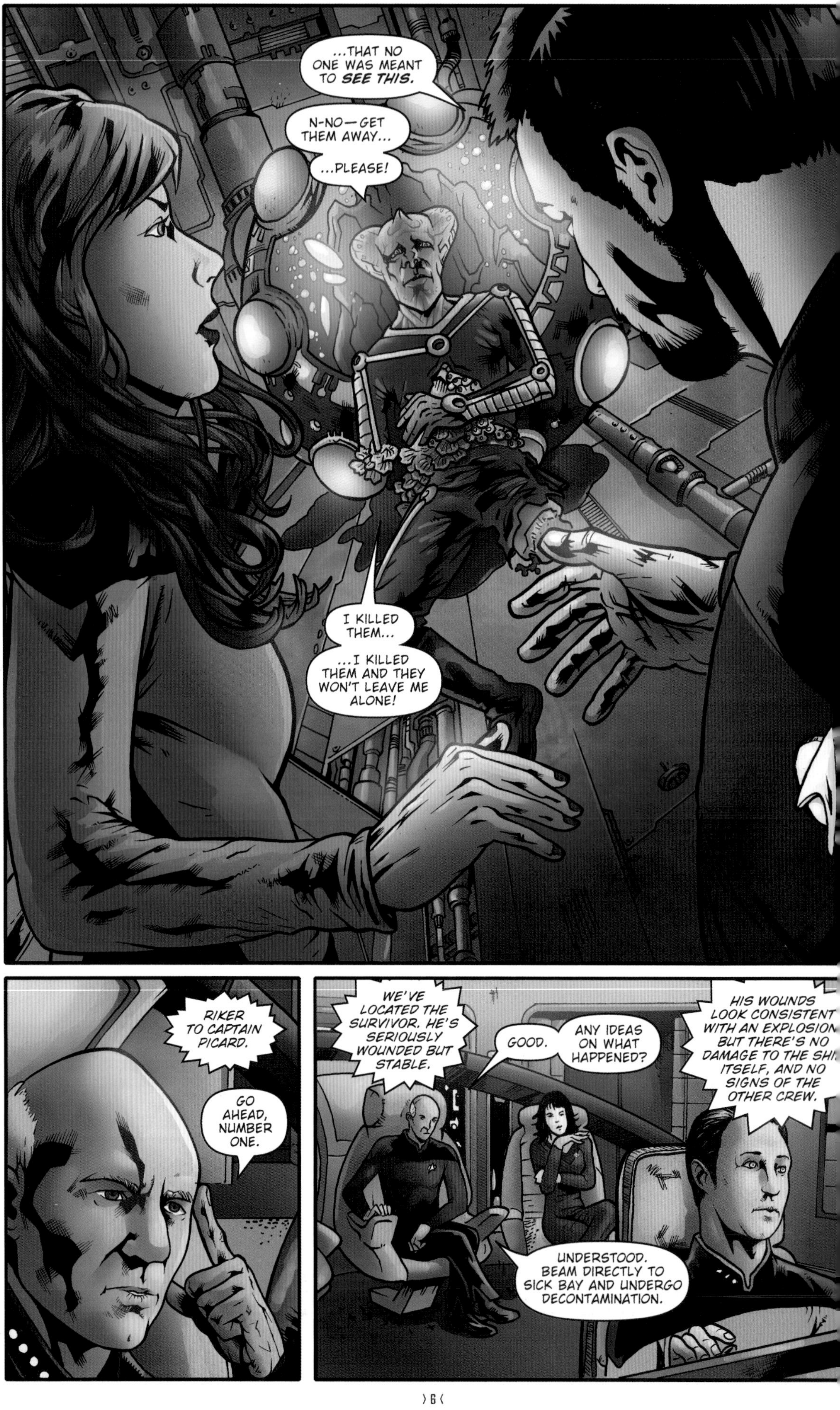

...THAT NO ONE WAS MEANT TO SEE THIS.
N-NO—GET THEM AWAY...
...PLEASE!
I KILLED THEM...
...I KILLED THEM AND THEY WON'T LEAVE ME ALONE!
RIKER TO CAPTAIN PICARD.
GO AHEAD, NUMBER ONE.
WE'VE LOCATED THE SURVIVOR. HE'S SERIOUSLY WOUNDED BUT STABLE.
GOOD.
ANY IDEAS ON WHAT HAPPENED?
HIS WOUNDS LOOK CONSISTENT WITH AN EXPLOSION BUT THERE'S NO DAMAGE TO THE SHI ITSELF, AND NO SIGNS OF THE OTHER CREW.
UNDERSTOOD. BEAM DIRECTLY TO SICK BAY AND UNDERGO DECONTAMINATION.

SIR, I RECOMMEND THAT LT. LA FORGE REMAIN ABOARD TO INVESTIGATE THE *CAUSE* OF THE EXPLOSION.

HMM. I WOULDN'T THINK THE JUULET COUNCIL WOULD LIKE THAT VERY MUCH, NUMBER ONE.

I'M SURE YOU'RE *RIGHT*, SIR.

VERY WELL, MAKE IT SO.

PICARD OUT.

CAPTAIN...

...I HATE TO PLAY DEVIL'S ADVOCATE, BUT WHY DO YOU WANT TO EXAMINE THE SHIP? THE SURVIVOR IS *SAFE*—

—AND THE JUULETIANS CAN ANALYZE THE SHIP *THEMSELVES.*

TRUE, COUNSELOR. I SUSPECT YOU'D SEE RIGHT THROUGH ME IF I SAID IT WAS JUST TO CHECK UP ON THE TRUTH OF THEIR *APPLICATION.*

I SUPPOSE IT'S... THESE RESEARCHERS ARE DOING WHAT WE DO, COUNSELOR, AND THEIR SUPERIORS SEEM QUITE CASUAL ABOUT THEIR DEATHS.

TO DIE WITH NO ONE TO SPEAK FOR YOU...

...THEY DESERVE *BETTER* THAN THAT.

IT'S VERY THOUGHTFUL OF YOU, CAPTA—

OH!

DEANNA?

COUNSELOR TROI, REPORT TO *SICK BAY.*

ON—ON MY *WAY.*

DEANNA, ARE YOU ALL RIGHT?

I—I'M OKAY...

SIR, WE ARE BEING *HAILED.*

IS IT THE JUULETIANS AGAIN?

NO, SIR.

THE HAIL IS USING AN OUTDATED FREQUENCY. THE SIGNAL REQUIRES SIGNIFICANT *CLEAN-UP.*

IT IS FROM THE NATION OF DOROSSH.

ON SCREEN.

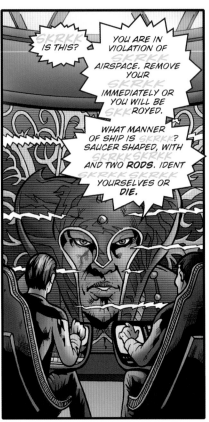

SKRKK IS THIS?

YOU ARE IN VIOLATION OF SKRKK AIRSPACE. REMOVE YOUR SKRKK IMMEDIATELY OR YOU WILL BE SKK ROYED.

WHAT MANNER OF SHIP IS SKRKK? SAUCER SHAPED, WITH SKRKKSKRKK AND TWO RODS. IDENT SKRKKSKRKK YOURSELVES OR DIE.

HAVE THEY NEVER SEEN A FEDERATION SHIP BEFORE?

THEIR WEAPONS HAVE LOCKED ONTO US, CAPTAIN.

IT IS A CLASS F BALLISTIC MISSILE. NO THREAT TO THE ENTERPRISE.

PEOPLE OF DOROSSH.

THIS IS CAPTAIN JEAN-LUC PICARD OF THE FEDERATION STARSHIP ENTERPRISE.

WE ARE IN THE PROCESS OF RESCUING A STRANDED SHIP IN ORBIT—WE ASK THAT YOU PLEASE PUT YOUR WEAPONS ON HOLD.

WE DO NOT SKRKK KNOW YOU, FEDERATION.

BUT A SHIP ABOVE US HAS BEEN SENT BY THE JUULETIAN *MURDERERS*, AND IF YOU *ASSIST* THEM—

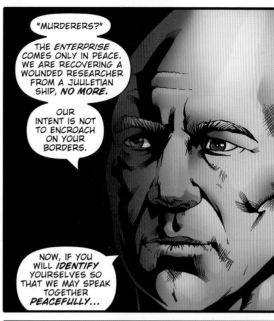

"MURDERERS?"

THE *ENTERPRISE* COMES ONLY IN PEACE. WE ARE RECOVERING A WOUNDED RESEARCHER FROM A JUULETIAN SHIP, *NO MORE*.

OUR INTENT IS NOT TO ENCROACH ON YOUR BORDERS.

NOW, IF YOU WILL *IDENTIFY* YOURSELVES SO THAT WE MAY SPEAK TOGETHER *PEACEFULLY*...

I AM SUPREME ELDER KALKASS, FEDERATION. I AM THE SOLE REMAIN SKRK ELDER, AND FOR THAT YOU MAY THANK YOUR DEAR SKRKK JUULETIANS.

BUT WE WILL NOT SPEAK ON THIS BROADCAST SHOUTING MACHINE, FEDERATION. THE *TOWER* IS THE ONLY PLACE FOR DISCUSSIONS OF WAR OR PEACE.

THE *TOWER*?

WHAT IS—

SKS ST

HE HAS ENDED THE TRANSMISSION, SIR.

MR. DATA, WHAT TOWER IS SUPREME ELDER KALKASS SPEAKING OF?

THE *TOWER* IS A LONG-UNUSED STRUCTURE ON THE BORDER BETWEEN JUULET AND DOROSSH, SIR.

IT WAS ONCE USED TO MEDIATE TALKS BETWEEN THE TWO NATIONS.

THE REPUBLIC OF *JUULET* CEASED USING IT ELEVEN YEARS AGO.

OF COURSE...

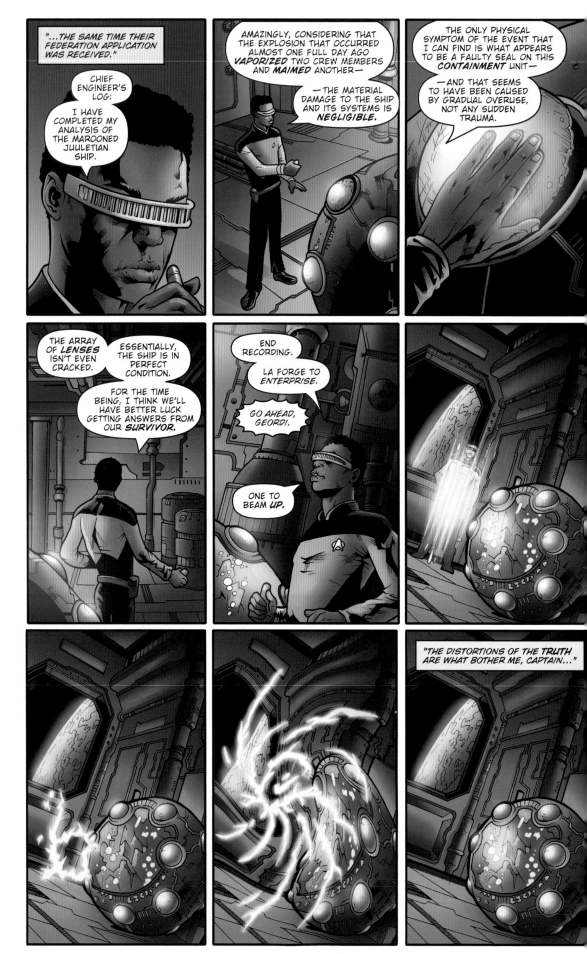

"...THE SAME TIME THEIR FEDERATION APPLICATION WAS RECEIVED."

CHIEF ENGINEER'S LOG:

I HAVE COMPLETED MY ANALYSIS OF THE MAROONED JUULETIAN SHIP.

AMAZINGLY, CONSIDERING THAT THE EXPLOSION THAT OCCURRED ALMOST ONE FULL DAY AGO *VAPORIZED* TWO CREW MEMBERS AND *MAIMED* ANOTHER—

—THE MATERIAL DAMAGE TO THE SHIP AND ITS SYSTEMS IS *NEGLIGIBLE.*

THE ONLY PHYSICAL SYMPTOM OF THE EVENT THAT I CAN FIND IS WHAT APPEARS TO BE A FAULTY SEAL ON THIS *CONTAINMENT* UNIT—

—AND THAT SEEMS TO HAVE BEEN CAUSED BY GRADUAL OVERUSE, NOT ANY SUDDEN TRAUMA.

THE ARRAY OF *LENSES* ISN'T EVEN CRACKED.

ESSENTIALLY, THE SHIP IS IN PERFECT CONDITION.

FOR THE TIME BEING, I THINK WE'LL HAVE BETTER LUCK GETTING ANSWERS FROM OUR *SURVIVOR.*

END RECORDING.

LA FORGE TO *ENTERPRISE.*

GO AHEAD, GEORDI.

ONE TO BEAM *UP.*

"THE DISTORTIONS OF THE *TRUTH* ARE WHAT BOTHER ME, CAPTAIN..."

YOUR POINT IS NOTED, NUMBER ONE, AND I *SHARE* IT, BUT...

...WE MUST GIVE THEM THE *CHANCE* TO TELL THEIR SIDE OF THE STORY.

SOUNDS LIKE THEY'VE BEEN TELLING THEIR SIDE FOR ELEVEN *YEARS.*

AGAIN, *NOTED.*

THAT'S PRECISELY WHY WE'LL MEET IN THE TOWER ON THE BORDER OF THE TWO COUNTRIES.

THE PEOPLE OF DOROSSH SEEM COMPLETELY UNAWARE OF THEIR PLANET'S CONSIDERATION FOR THE FEDERATION.

AT LEAST THIS MEETING WILL CORRECT *THAT.*

THE *ACCUSATIONS* ARE *ANOTHER* MATTER. PERHAPS THE *OPENNESS* THAT FEDERATION *MEMBERSHIP* REQUIRES WILL ENCOURAGE THEM TO SHED SOME *LIGHT* ON WHAT *KALKASS* HAS SAID.

HELLO, SIR. COMMANDER. THE SPEAKER OF JUULET HAS SENT COORDINATES FOR THEIR PALACE.

WE WON'T BE NEEDING THEM, O'BRIEN.

NO?

PUT US INTO THE TOWER THAT SITS ON THE WALL BETWEEN THE TWO COUNTRIES.

YES, SIR, LOCATING...

NUMBER ONE, WHAT IS THE STATUS OF THE SURVIVOR?

CONSIDERING THE EXTENT OF HIS INJURIES, SIR, HE'S DOING *WELL.* DR. CRUSHER HASN'T FOUND ANY INFECTION AND HIS SIGNS ARE *STABLE.*

THE PROBLEM IS HIS *MIND.*

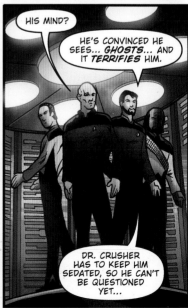

HIS MIND?

HE'S CONVINCED HE SEES... *GHOSTS...* AND IT *TERRIFIES* HIM.

DR. CRUSHER HAS TO KEEP HIM SEDATED, SO HE CAN'T BE QUESTIONED YET...

"...IT'S SILENCE OR LUNACY AT THIS POINT."

REALLY, CAPTAIN PICARD...

...FOR DISCUSSIONS OF *JUULET* AND THE *FEDERATION*, WE HAVE *MUCH* MORE COMFORTABLE ACCOMMODATIONS WITHIN THE *CITY*.

I'M SURE YOU DO, SPEAKER KEJAAL.

BUT, AS YOU KNOW, THE FEDERATION DOES NOT OFFER MEMBERSHIP TO *NATIONS.*

JUST *PLANETS.*

OH, WELL, *CAPTAIN, NATURALLY.* BUT THE REPUBLIC OF JUULET REPRESENTS THE INTERESTS OF *ALL* OF ALLIOS IV...

YOU *MAY*, OF COURSE, BUT THERE IS A LARGE PERCENTAGE OF ALLIOS IV...

...THAT HAS BEEN LEFT OUT OF THIS DISCUSSION.

OH, COME NOW, CAPTAIN, THE *DOROSSHIANS*? THERE HASN'T BEEN A GOVERNMENT SITTING THERE FOR YEA—

LIES!

IF HE SPEAKS, IT IS A *LIE!*

THESE JUULETIAN *DEVILS*—!

—THEY DEFILE THIS *SACRED PLACE!*

CAPTAIN, NO! THESE MEN—

—THEY ARE SIMPLY LOCAL *STRONGMEN* WHO HAVE JUST *KILLED* THEIR WAY TO PROMINENCE!

BAH! YOUR ONE FINGER POINTS AT ME—FOUR MORE POINT BACK AT YOU, BUTCHER!

EVERYONE, EVERYONE, *PLEASE.*

THIS IS A PLACE OF *PEACE*, IS IT *NOT?* LET US CONVENE *FORMALLY* AT THE TABLE AND SURELY WE CAN ADDRESS *EVERYONE'S* CONCERNS.

PLEASE...

FOR THE SAKE OF YOUR PLANET'S *HISTORY*...

...AND OF ITS *FUTURE.*

CAPTAIN'S LOG, SUPPLEMENTAL.

WE HAVE CONVINCED THE WARRING JUULETIANS AND DOROSSHIANS TO SIT AND DISCUSS THEIR DIFFERENCES AT A TRADITIONAL NEUTRAL LOCATION: THE *TOWER*.

IT IS DIFFICULT TO CONVINCE EITHER SIDE THAT THIS MEETING IS IN THEIR *INTERESTS*. BUT I SUSPECT THAT APPEALING TO THE FEDERATION'S SENSE OF *FAIRNESS* ON THE ONE HAND AND ITS *POWER* ON THE OTHER INTRIGUES *EACH* OF THEM TO VARYING DEGREES.

I HAVE BROUGHT THEM UP TO DATE ON THE STATUS OF THE SURVIVOR OF THE EXPLOSION.

uul everuud

THE JUULETIANS HAVE IDENTIFIED HIM AS A RESEARCHER NAMED *UUL EVERUUD*.

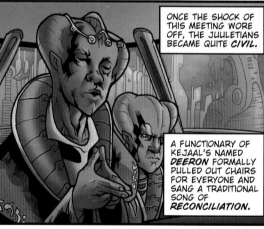

ONCE THE SHOCK OF THIS MEETING WORE OFF, THE JUULETIANS BECAME QUITE *CIVIL*.

A FUNCTIONARY OF KEJAAL'S NAMED *DEERON* FORMALLY PULLED OUT CHAIRS FOR EVERYONE AND SANG A TRADITIONAL SONG OF *RECONCILIATION*.

I WISH THE SAME COULD BE SAID OF THE *DOROSSHIANS*.

SUPREME ELDER *KALKASS* HAS BEEN *DISRUPTIVE*, AND HIS DAUGHTER, *WORIKK*, HAS REFUSED TO ANSWER EVEN SIMPLE QUESTIONS.

AS WE MOVE INTO MORE SPECIFIC MATTERS ABOUT THE SHIP AND ITS LOCATION, THE CONVERSATION BECAME MORE AND MORE HEATED, AND *PERSONAL*.

A RESEARCH VESSEL?!

THESE JUULETIAN MEN-WHO-SPEAK-LIKE-WOMEN THINK WE ARE CREDULOUS CHILDREN, *FEDERATION!*

IT IS A WEAPON AIMED AT OUR *HEARTS!*

RIDICULOUS. CAPTAIN PICARD, THESE ACCUSATIONS ARE *BASELESS*, LIKE THEIR CLAIMS OF *SOVEREIGNTY*.

OUR SHIP HAS NO *WEAPONS*, AS YOUR *AWAY TEAM* CAN *ATTEST*.

SUPREME ELDER, COMMANDER RIKER WAS ABOARD THE SHIP, HE REPORTED NO WEAPONS.

YES, THAT'S *TRUE*.

BUT I—

IT DOES NOT *MATTER!* THE SHIP IS *JUULETIAN!*

WORIKK?

IF IT WERE ONLY A LITTLE BIT *BIGGER* WE WOULD HAVE BLASTED IT FROM THE SKY—

—NO MATTER *WHAT* ITS PURPOSE!

IDIOT! OXYGEN-DEPRIVED INFANT!

FOOL!

SMACK

OW! FATHER!

WILL YOU TELL ALL OUR LIMITATIONS?

AH...

...SUPREME ELDER KALKASS, PERHAPS NOW WOULD BE A TIME FOR A SHORT RECESS...

NO.

ALL SIX OF MY FELLOW ELDERS HAVE VANISHED IN THE PAST TWO YEARS, FEDERATION.

THESE ASSASSINS AND THEIR SHIP ARE TO *BLAME*.

DO YOU HAVE ANY PROOF OF THIS, ELDER KALKASS?

÷SIGH÷

CAPTAIN, OF COURSE HE DOESN'T...

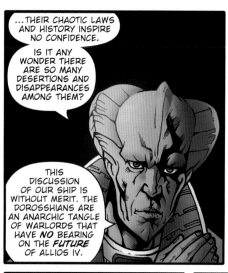

...THEIR CHAOTIC LAWS AND HISTORY INSPIRE NO CONFIDENCE.

IS IT ANY WONDER THERE ARE SO MANY DESERTIONS AND DISAPPEARANCES AMONG THEM?

THIS DISCUSSION OF OUR SHIP IS WITHOUT MERIT. THE DOROSSHIANS ARE AN ANARCHIC TANGLE OF WARLORDS THAT HAVE **NO** BEARING ON THE **FUTURE** OF ALLIOS IV.

I MOVE WE CONTINUE THE DISCUSSION OF OUR APPLICATION TO THE FEDERATION **BACK** INTO OUR CAPITOL PALACE, AND—

ONE MOMENT, SPEAKER KEJAAL.

THERE WERE NO WEAPONS ABOARD YOUR SHIP, TRUE...

...BUT THE VIEWPORTS HAD AN ELABORATE ARRAY OF LENSES...

...AIMED DIRECTLY AT THE DOROSSHIANS.

CAN YOU **EXPLAIN** THAT?

—SIGH—

COMMANDER—

HA! AS WE SAID—**A WEAPON!**

A **SURVEILLANCE** SHIP, KALKASS.

IT IS SIMPLY A **SURVEILLANCE** SHIP.

CAN YOU BLAME US, CAPTAIN **PICARD?** COMMANDER **RIKER?** **THESE** ARE OUR NEIGHBORS...

...AND ALL THAT SEPARATES US IS SOME THIN **WALL...**

...AND THE **DOZENS** OF BROKEN PROMISES THEY HAVE LEFT US WITH IN **THIS ROOM.**

PROMISES OF **DISARMAMENT.**

PROMISES OF **SCHOOLS.**

PROMISES OF EQUITABLE DISTRIBUTION OF **SOPPAN LIQUID.**

ALL IN TREATIES SIGNED OVER **DECADES...**

...AND ALL **IGNORED.**

SO **CERTAINLY** WE WATCH THEM.

AND IT MAY WELL SEEM A HOSTILE ACT, BUT TO **WATCH** AND **LISTEN** FOR WAR IS NOT TO **WAGE** IT.

HMPH. "PROMISES."

ELDER KALKASS, IS WHAT SPEAKER KEJAAL SAYS *TRUE?*

BAH.

THEIR WEAKNESS SHOWS IN THEIR... *REQUIREMENT* OF SUCH NICETIES.

HMM.

PERHAPS WE MIGHT RETIRE FOR TODAY AND PICK UP AGAIN TOMORROW.

CAPTAIN...

...WHEN WILL WE BE ABLE TO RECEIVE RESEARCHER EVERUUD?

HIS ACCOUNT OF THE DISASTER WILL PROVIDE VALUABLE DATA TO OUR SHUTTLE CREW.

I'M AFRAID IT WON'T BE POSSIBLE TO RETURN HIM UNTIL OUR MEDICAL OFFICER HAS DONE A FEW MORE SCANS.

I'M SORRY FOR THE DELAY, BUT WE'D LIKE TO BE THOROUGH.

AND *US,* FEDERATION?

WILL YOU DO WHAT *WE* DEMAND, AND MOVE THIS GUNSHIP OUT OF OUR *SKY?*

NO. WE WILL NOT.

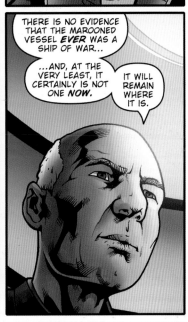

THERE IS NO EVIDENCE THAT THE MAROONED VESSEL *EVER* WAS A SHIP OF WAR...

...AND, AT THE VERY LEAST, IT CERTAINLY IS NOT ONE *NOW.*

IT WILL REMAIN WHERE IT IS.

NOW, IN PREPARATION FOR TOMORROW'S MEETING, WE WISH TO TASK SOME OF OUR CREW TO ACT AS *LIAISONS* WITH YOUR COUNTRIES.

BUT—

FURTHER STUDY OF YOUR CULTURES WILL HELP SPEED THE APPLICATION PROCESS.

"STUDY."

"DELAY."

THESE "LIAISONS."

THIS IS NOT *DECISION,* FEDERATION—

—IT IS *NOTHING.*

YOU HAVE TAKEN NO ACTION, *CAPTAIN—*

"—AND WHO BUT A *DEAD MAN* TAKES NO *ACTION*?"

I CAN'T BELIEVE YOU'RE TELLING ME THIS ISN'T AS BAD AS IT LOOKS.

WELL, IT'S CERTAINLY *BAD.*

BUT THIS GLOW AROUND HIS WOUNDS—IT'S NOT AN ENERGY SIGNATURE WE'VE EVER RUN INTO BEFORE.

WHATEVER CAUSED IT SEEMS TO HAVE CAUTERIZED HIS WOUNDS AND HAS COMPLETELY PROTECTED HIM FROM ANY OPPORTUNISTIC INFECTIONS.

CAUTERIZED?

YES, THE ENERGY HAS SEALED OFF THE WOUND...

...LIKE A MAKESHIFT SKIN.

BUT IN *THIS* CASE, INSTEAD OF CAUSING MASSIVE DAMAGE, AS BURNS FROM *FIRE* OR *TORIALIS* ENERGY DO...

...THE TISSUE REMAINS *ALIVE*—NOT DRYING, NOT HEALING, JUST *ALIVE.*

AS IF... IT WERE STILL *INSIDE* THE BODY, NOT EXPOSED TO *AIR.*

DOCTOR CRUSHER. THE HIGH-DENSITY SCANS OF THE *WOUNDS* ARE IN.

GOOD, THANK YOU, XIAN.

CAN YOU SEND THE RESULTS TO THIS *STATION*?

I CAN'T *BELIEVE* THIS.

WHAT DO YOU *SEE*?

THESE SCANS ON THE CELLULAR LEVEL...

...IN THIS IMAGE OF THE WOUND'S SURFACE, THESE *CAROLUS* CELLS, THE EQUIVALENT TO OUR RED BLOOD CELLS, ARE ACTUALLY SLICED IN HALF BY THE EXPLOSION'S ENERGY.

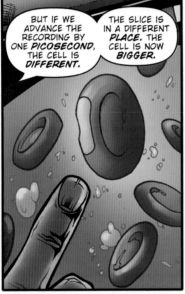

BUT IF WE ADVANCE THE RECORDING BY ONE *PICOSECOND*, THE CELL IS *DIFFERENT*.

THE SLICE IS IN A DIFFERENT *PLACE*. THE CELL IS NOW *BIGGER*.

WHAT DOES THAT *MEAN*?

I DON'T KNOW... IT'S LIKE THE ADDITIONAL *MASS* IS COMING FROM SOMEWHERE ELS—

BEE-BEEP

BEVERLY, HE'S COMING OUT OF SEDATION.

RESEARCHER *EVERUUD*?

UUL?

NH?

UUL, CAN YOU HEAR ME?

NH... K-KEER?

KEER? I-IS THAT Y—

OH, NO— OH WH-WHERE *AM I??*

SHH... SHH... YOU'RE *SAFE.*

YOU'RE ON THE FEDERATION STARSHIP *ENTERP*—

NO!

WHY? WHY ARE THEY HERE?

THEY'RE STILL *HERE!*

TH-THE *GHOSTS!*

IT'S ALL RIGHT!

UUL, IT'S ALL RIGHT!

SHH... SHH...

NO... NO, I CAN'T...

PLEASE...

TH-THEY JUST WON'T GO AWAY...

DOCTOR—

I KNOW, HE'S BEEN LIKE THIS SINCE WE BROUGHT HIM BACK.

N-NO...

I'D HOPED THAT YOU COULD CALM HIM *DOWN.*

IT SEEMS TO HAVE WORKED. AT LEAST A *LITTLE.*

PERHAPS, BUT I DON'T KNOW IF I'LL GET MUCH OUT OF HIM.

HE'S *TERRIFIED,* BUT MORE THAN THAT, HE'S COMPLETELY *CONFUSED.*

HIS SENSES ARE OVERWHELMED WITH... *SOMETHING.*

SOMETHING WE CAN'T SEE, OR EVEN SENSE.

YES, I NEED TO LOOK *INTO* THIS SOME MORE... MAYBE *GEORDI* WILL HAVE SOME INSIGHT.

TELL XIAN IF YOU FEEL HE NEEDS TO BE SEDATED AGAIN.

CRUSHER TO LA FORGE.

GO AHEAD, DOCTOR.

WELL, GEORDI...

"...I'VE GOT QUITE A *MYSTERY* FOR YOU."

OKAY...

...SO YOU THINK THAT THIS ENERGY HAS CREATED A *FIELD* OF SOME KIND THAT...

...WHAT, *SHIFTS* THINGS INTO OTHER *DIMENSIONS*?

I DON'T KNOW— I MEAN, WE DON'T EVEN KNOW WHAT THIS ENERGY IS, RIGHT?

IT DOESN'T EVEN SHOW UP ON OUR *SENSORS*.

OR... IT *DOES*, BUT THE SENSORS DON'T KNOW HOW TO INTERPRET IT.

HMM.

COMPUTER.

LIST ALL KNOWN ENERGIES THAT HAVE A *PHASE-SHIFTING* EFFECT.

THERE ARE 725 KNOWN ENERGIES WITH THAT EFFECT.

ALL RIGHT, HOW MANY OF THOSE WOULD NOT SHOW UP ON A STANDARD SCAN—OR A TRICORDER?

377.

AND PRODUCES A WHITE GLOW IN FLESH EXPOSED TO IT?

26.

HOW MANY OF THOSE HAVE BEEN OBSERVED IN THIS SECTOR?

4.

LIST AND SEND TO THIS TERMINAL.

BEVERLY, LOOK AT *THIS*.

LOOKS LIKE WE FOUND THE *CULPRIT*.

1. STWALLIAN GLOW FOUND: ZARC 113 CLOUD
2. GAALAN EMANATA FOUND: EDGE OF F NEB
3. ZOOR ENERGY FOUND: CORE OF ALL
4. DOW BEAMS FOUND: 66804

HMM. CAN YOU ADJUST THE *TRICORDERS* TO READ IT?

SURE, I'LL RETUNE THE *SHIP'S* SENSORS, TOO.

TROUBLE *IS*, WHERE DOES THAT *GET* US?

AND MORE IMPORTANTLY, HOW DO WE FIX IT?

RIGHT, I—

PICARD TO DR. CRUSHER.

GO AHEAD, CAPTAIN.

PLEASE REPORT TO *SICK BAY.* I'D LIKE TO SPEAK WITH OUR *SURVIVOR.*

ON MY WAY.

THANKS, GEORDI.

NO PROBLEM. I'LL BE BY TO RETUNE THE MEDICAL TRICORDERS.

HOW WAS THE MEETING?

⸻SIGH⸻ *TRYING.*

I'M NOT SURE WHY EACH SIDE HAS TO MAKE IT SO *DIFFICULT,* OR...

...OR WHY YOU HAVE TO *CARE* SO MUCH?

HMM. *I SUPPOSE.*

IT'S REALLY NONE OF OUR *CONCERN* WHETHER ALLIOS IS LET INTO THE FEDERATION OR NOT...

...BUT I JUST WANT TO SORT OUT EVERYONE'S *STORIES* AND FIND OUT WHAT HAPPENED TO THE *SHIP,* THEN MOVE *ON.*

WHY MUST PEOPLE MAKE IT HARD FOR THE TRUTH TO COME OUT?

ALL THIS *BLUSTER,* AND ALL THESE EVASIONS, JUST MAKE ME FEEL *DEAD* INSIDE.

WELL, SIR, GEORDI AND I MAY HAVE FIGURED OUT ONE ASPECT OF THE SHIP DISASTER.

DOES IT TELL US WHETHER OR NOT THE SHIP HAD *WEAPONS?*

AH, ACTUALLY, THERE'S SOME EVIDENCE THAT THEY INTENTIONALLY BROUGHT UP THE ELEMENT THAT *CAUSED* THE EXPLOSION, BUT...

YES, WELL, LET'S ASK THE SURVIVOR WHAT HE KNOWS—I'D LIKE TO GO INTO TOMORROW'S MEETING WITH SOME SOLID INFORMATION, IF I CAN.

COUNSELOR TROI IS SPEAKING WITH RESEARCHER EVERUUD RIGHT NOW.

HE'S BEEN DIFFICULT TO COMMUNICATE WITH, AS WILL MUST HAVE TOLD YOU.

YES... THESE... *HALLUCINATIONS*. OF *DEAD PEOPLE*.

YES, BUT NOW, *CAPTAIN*, IF GEORDI AND I ARE *CORRECT*...

...WE MAY BE DEALING WITH A DIMENSIONAL SHIFT THAT'S *SPECIFIC* TO THE SURVIVOR. BASICALLY—

—THEY MAY NOT *BE* HALLUCINATIONS.

THE GHOSTS MAY BE *REAL*.

HMM. ALL RIGHT.

HERE WE ARE.

I—THE UM... THEY'RE *TALKING* TO ME. I-I JUST... CAN'T UNDERSTAND WHAT THEY *WANT*—

BUT WHO *ARE* THEY?

DO YOU KNOW ANY OF THEM? FRIENDS?

I-IT'S TOO HARD TO *SEE*... I DON'T *KNOW*...

COUNSELOR.

CAPTAIN. LET ME INTRODUCE YOU TO OUR SURVIVOR, *UUL EVERUUD*.

PLEASED TO—

NO!

NNO!

YOU! WHAT ARE YOU DOING HERE?!

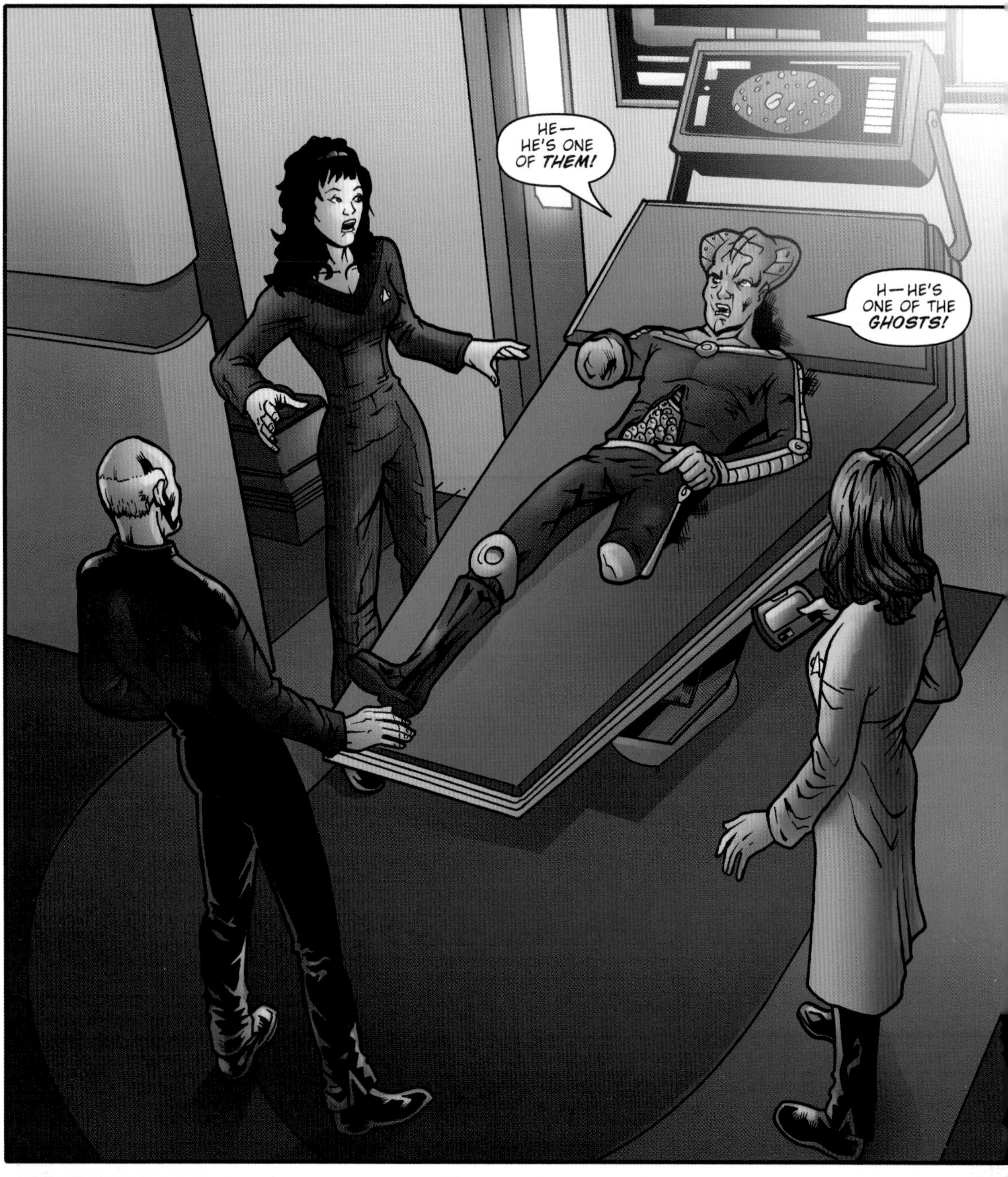
HE—
HE'S ONE
OF THEM!
H—HE'S
ONE OF THE
GHOSTS!

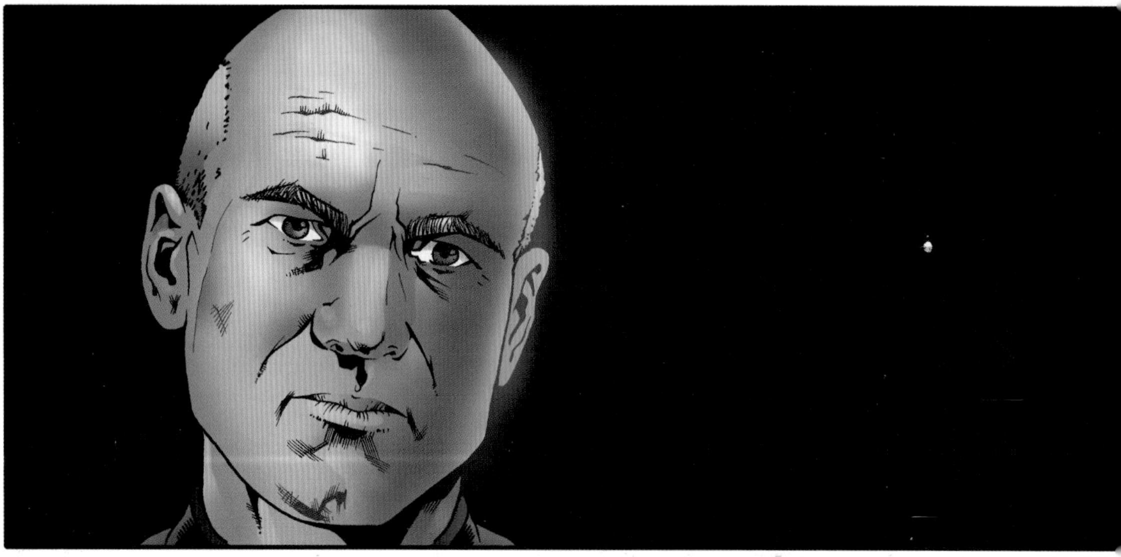

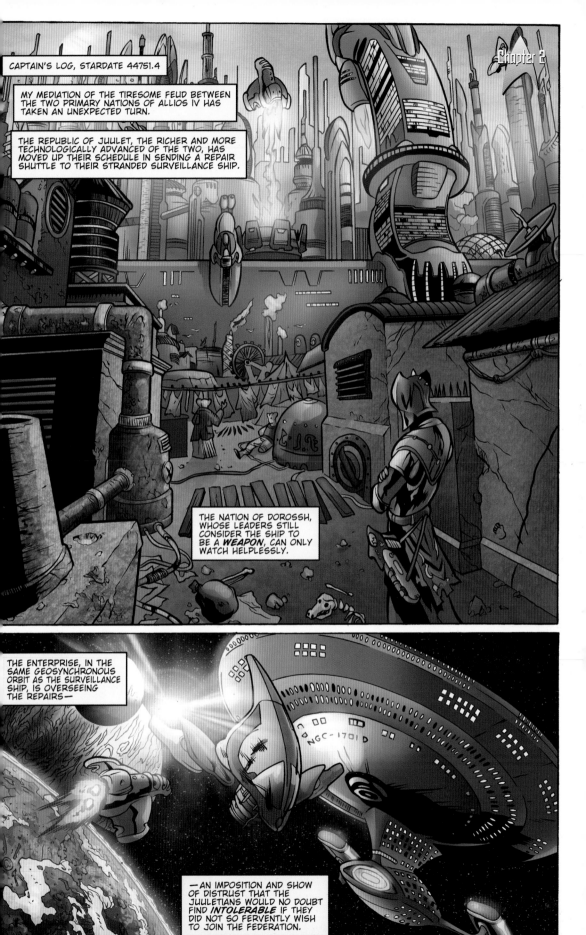

Chapter 2

CAPTAIN'S LOG, STARDATE 44751.4

MY MEDIATION OF THE TIRESOME FEUD BETWEEN THE TWO PRIMARY NATIONS OF ALLIOS IV HAS TAKEN AN UNEXPECTED TURN.

THE REPUBLIC OF JUULET, THE RICHER AND MORE TECHNOLOGICALLY ADVANCED OF THE TWO, HAS MOVED UP THEIR SCHEDULE IN SENDING A REPAIR SHUTTLE TO THEIR STRANDED SURVEILLANCE SHIP.

THE NATION OF DOROSSH, WHOSE LEADERS STILL CONSIDER THE SHIP TO BE A *WEAPON*, CAN ONLY WATCH HELPLESSLY.

THE ENTERPRISE, IN THE SAME GEOSYNCHRONOUS ORBIT AS THE SURVEILLANCE SHIP, IS OVERSEEING THE REPAIRS—

NGC-1701-D

—AN IMPOSITION AND SHOW OF DISTRUST THAT THE JUULETIANS WOULD NO DOUBT FIND *INTOLERABLE* IF THEY DID NOT SO FERVENTLY WISH TO JOIN THE FEDERATION.

I HAVE DISPATCHED COMMANDER DATA AND LIEUTENANT WORF TO INVESTIGATE THE HISTORIES AND CLAIMS OF JUULET AND DOROSSH, RESPECTIVELY.

I SURMISE THAT THEIR TEMPERAMENTS WILL SUIT THEM TO THE CHOSEN COUNTRIES.

WITH THAT—AND THE TREATMENT OF THE SURVEILLANCE SHIP'S SOLE SURVIVOR PROGRESSING APACE—WE HAVE A RARE QUIET MOMENT ABOARD THE ENTERPRISE.

BEEBOOP

COME.

HELLO, CAPTAIN.

COUNSELOR!

AH... WHAT BRINGS *YOU* HERE?

IS THE PATIENT CONTINUING TO BE LESS-THAN-FORTHCOMING ABOUT THESE... *HALLUCINATIONS* HE SEES?

WELL, HE'S ASLEEP—*SEDATED.* HE STILL FEELS SO *CONFUSED.* HE CAN'T CONCENTRATE LONG ENOUGH TO TELL US ANYTHING.

BUT IT WAS *YOUR* EMOTIONS THAT BROUGHT ME HERE, SIR.

MY EMOTIONS?

IT SEEMS THAT YOU'VE EXPERIENCED SOME DARK THOUGHTS SINCE YOUR ENCOUNTER WITH OUR PATIENT, CAPTAIN.

WHAT? OH, NO, *NONSENSE.*

JUST A MOMENT OF *REFLECTION.*

SIR—BEING SINGLED OUT BY RESEARCHER EVERUUD AS ONE OF THE... PEOPLE THAT ARE *HAUNTING* HIM...

...THAT COULD MAKE ONE FAIRLY INTROSPECTIVE.

THOUGHTS OF *MORTALITY*... OF *FINALITY*...

COUNSELOR, I APPRECIATE YOUR CONCERN, I REALLY DO, BUT...

...IT'S JUST THAT IT'S BEEN A *WEARYING* THIRTY-SOME HOURS HERE.

I'M *PERFECTLY* FINE.

YOU CAN LEAVE ME HERE WITH MY DARK THOUGHTS.

THIS ONE: DELBBAN WAS HIS FATHER, HE HAD NO HEIR. HE DIED FOUR QUADS PAST.

HIS NAME WAS POLKKAR.

AND THIS ONE: OQQUN WAS HIS FATHER, DUWWOR WAS HIS HEIR. HE DIED SIX QUADS PAST.

HIS NAME WAS MMEMON.

THIS ONE: SOXXAL WAS HIS FATHER, MANNEX IS HIS HEIR, STILL AN INFANT. HE DIED TWENTY-TWO CYCLES PAST.

HIS NAME—

ER, YES, ONE MOMENT, ELDER KALKASS—

OF COURSE THIS IS FASCINATING, SIR...

...BUT THE HISTORY I'M HERE TO REVIEW IS MEANT TO BE... THE STORIES OF ALL OF YOUR PEOPLE.

BAH.

WHY WOULD YOUR FEDERATION *CARE* ABOUT THE TREACHEROUS FAILED USURPERS AND ADDICTED FOOLS, KLINGON?

THE DEEDS OF THE MIGHTY AND WISE ELDERS ARE THE SOIL OUR DOROSSH HAVE SPRUNG FROM.

JUST LOOKING UPON THE FACES OF THESE DEAD KINGS TELLS YOU OUR HISTORY.

A HISTORY OF HEROES, OF CONQUERORS, OF... OF... MARTYRS...

...OF...

...OF...

⫶SIGH⫶

BAH.

WE HAVE SPENT ENOUGH TIME HERE, WITH THESE OLD STORIES.

COME.

FOR A FULL HISTORY...

...YOU WILL WANT TO SEE **VOLMOLOKK**, THE SINGER. HE IS ON THE FAR SIDE OF—

=GROAN=

FATHER...

WHAT IS IT, WORIKK, YOU LAZY CHILD?

VOLMOLOKK IS TOO *OLD!* HE IS A FOOL WHO ONLY THINKS OF THE OLD DAYS!

BAH.

IF ONLY *YOU* WOULD THINK OF THE OLD DAYS...

...INSTEAD OF WISHING FOR THINGS YOU CANNOT HAVE. THEN YOU MIGHT BE AN ELDER ONE DAY.

AN *UNLIKELY* OUTCOME AT *BEST.*

WH—?

YOU SEE, FEDERATION, WHAT I MUST CONTEND WITH? I, THE LAST ELDER? AN HEIR THAT IS A FOOL! THESE INFERNAL JUULETIANS AND THEIR LIES!

IT'S...

...IT'S ENOUGH TO MAKE ME WISH THAT GUN IN THE SKY WOULD JUST TAKE ME TOO.

THE DOROSSH I KNOW IS LONG *GONE.* DEAD WITH THE *OTHER* ELDERS.

IF IT WERE A CHOICE BETWEEN RAISING A CUP WITH OLD FRIENDS IN OUR WARRIOR HEAVEN AND LISTENING TO IDIOTS AND ASSASSINS...

...IT WOULD BE NO CHOICE AT ALL.

GO TALK TO VOLMOLOKK, FEDERATION. HE WILL TELL YOU HOW WE CAME TO THIS SORRY *STATE.*

I'M *TIRED.*

THE OLD *FOSSIL—*

HE KNOWS *NOTHING* OF WHAT MUST BE DONE TO KEEP DOROSSH MOVING. *NOTHING.*

WORIKK, WHAT—

HE KNEW ALL THE ELDERS, AND SO USED TO ACCOMPLISH WHAT HAD TO BE DONE THAT WAY.

...BUT NOW THAT THE ELDERS ARE *DEAD,* AND THIS IS A *NEW* TIME, HE IS JUST A *RELIC.*

SEE, FEDERATION? HE STILL WEARS THE SAME ARMOR FROM THAT MEETING WITH YOUR *JUULETIANS* YESTERDAY.

THE DUST AND DETRITUS FROM THEIR CUSHIONED CHAIRS IS STILL ON HIS *BACKSIDE.*

LOOK AT HIM.

HE IS *RIDICULOUS,* A CLOWN WHOSE WORLD HAS—

WORIKK, *PLEASE.*

YOUR FATHER MAY BE *HARD* ON YOU, BUT YOU MUST NOT SPEAK OF HIM LIKE THIS.

YOU ARE A *WARRIOR PEOPLE*, AND RESPECT FOR ONE'S FATHER IS THE WARRIOR'S *WAY*.

HAH.

PERHAPS FOR WHAT PASSES FOR WARRIORS IN YOUR FEDERATION, IT IS THE WARRIOR'S WAY.

YOU MAY BE SENTIMENTAL IN YOUR *HOUSES-IN-THE-SKY*.

THEY ALLOW YOU TO FLOAT ABOVE US IN *JUDGMENT*...

...WHILE EVERYTHING YOU WANT IS PLACED IN YOUR MOUTHS BY YOUR *OVERLORDS*.

NOT LIKE US. NOT LIKE *DOROSSH*.

WHERE WE FOUGHT FOR EVERYTHING WE OWN...

...AND THEN FOUGHT AGAIN TO KEEP IT.

MM

WORIKK, LET ME TELL YOU *THIS*.

I KNOW SOMETHING OF LOSS...

...AND THE LOSS OF A FATHER YOU HAVE MALIGNED AND DISRESPECTED IS IMPOSSIBLE TO BEAR.

IT IS A MARK OF SHAME ON *ANY* WARRIOR, NO MATTER HIS OR HER ORIGIN.

YOU HAVE INSULTED ME, WORIKK...

...AND NORMALLY I WOULD SEEK TO SETTLE SUCH AN INSULT HERE, ON THESE DESERTED STREETS.

BUT MY SUPERIORS HAVE REQUESTED I PERFORM AN AUDIT OF YOUR NATION'S HISTORY.

SO I WILL DO THAT.

BUT KNOW THIS—FROM ONE HEIR TO ANOTHER—NOTHING IS FOREVER. MUCH AS WE THINK IT CAN NEVER HAPPEN, WORIKK...

...FATHERS EVENTUALLY DIE.

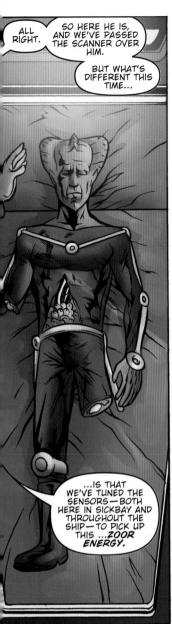

ALL RIGHT.

SO HERE HE IS, AND WE'VE PASSED THE SCANNER OVER HIM.

BUT WHAT'S DIFFERENT THIS TIME...

...IS THAT WE'VE TUNED THE SENSORS—BOTH HERE IN SICKBAY AND THROUGHOUT THE SHIP—TO PICK UP THIS ...*ZOOR ENERGY*.

OF COURSE, YOU CAN SEE THE WHITE GLOW AROUND HIS WOUNDS WITH NO ENHANCEMENT AT ALL.

BUT IF WE ADJUST THE FILTER LIKE SO...

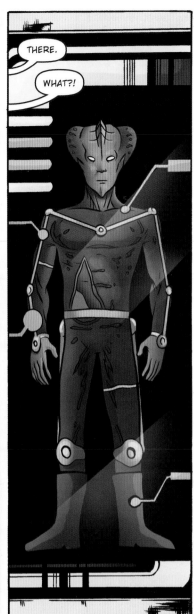

THERE.

WHAT?!

GEORDI— HE'S *COMPLETE*. IT'S LIKE HE HASN'T BEEN MAIMED AT *ALL*.

BUT HIS *LIMBS*—

—WHERE ARE THEY?

THAT I DON'T KNOW.

WE DON'T KNOW MUCH ABOUT THIS ENERGY OTHER THAN THE ORE THAT PRODUCES IT IS MINED FROM THE CORE OF THE PLANET.

SO THEY COULD BE... IN ANOTHER SPACE, WITH THIS ENERGY SIGNATURE OUR ONLY LINK TO THEM.

OR THE SIGNATURE COULD BE A MERE *APPROXIMATION* OF THE LIMBS IT DESTROYED, AND...

...AND HE REALLY DID KILL THEM ALL.

WHAT DO YOU *MEAN*, DEANNA?

AS HE SAID WHEN YOU *FOUND* HIM. "I KILLED THEM ALL, AND THEY WON'T LEAVE ME *ALONE*."

THIS BEAM THAT INJURED HIM—IT MUST HAVE KILLED THE OTHER TWO SCIENTISTS ABOARD THE SHIP.

AND OTHERS, TOO—ALL THE ACCIDENTS WITH THIS ORE OVER THE YEARS...

...PERHAPS EVEN IN THE *FUTURE*.

THE ENERGY IS SOME HOW LINKING HIM TO THEM...

...AND HE CAN PERCEIVE WHAT IS TOO SUBTLE EVEN FOR THE *TRICORDERS*.

IT'S HIS *GUILT*. HIS *GUILT* LETS HIM SEE WHAT WE *CAN'T*.

HM. I DON'T KNOW IF I *BUY* THAT, COUNSELOR.

I MEAN, GUILT'S *POWERFUL*, BUT AS FOR SEEING *THINGS*?

I'LL TAKE MY *VISOR* ANY DAY.

WELL...

BRIDGE TO LA FORGE.

LA FORGE HERE, COMMANDER. GO **AHEAD**.

GEORDI, OUR SENSORS PICKED UP A BIG SPIKE OF THAT ENERGY YOU WERE TALKING ABOUT.

WHAT? FROM **WHERE**?

IT'S FROM THE JUULETIAN **SURVEILLANCE** SHIP.

COMMANDER, MY SCHEDULE SAYS NO ONE'S DUE ABOARD UNTIL 1400 HOURS.

-:SIGH:- YES, MINE TOO.

I CAN'T BELIEVE THEY'D JUMP THE GUN LIKE THIS WHEN THEY'RE SO HUNGRY FOR FEDERATION APPROVAL, COMMANDER.

DEANNA? ARE YOU ALL **RIGHT**?

YES, I...

I'M **FINE**. I JUST—I FEEL A LITTLE HELPLESS. I WENT TO SEE THE **CAPTAIN** EARLIER...

...AND HE STILL WON'T COME DOWN AND SPEAK WITH OUR **SURVIVOR**?

IT'S MORE THAN THAT. HE HAS SUCH DARK FEELINGS ABOUT BEING SEEN AS A GHOST— FEELINGS THAT HE WON'T ACKNOWLEDGE.

WHATEVER IT MEANS TO OUR **MYSTERY**, HE NEEDS TO FACE HIS FEARS, FOR HIS OWN SAKE.

WELL, DEANNA, I AGREE, BUT IT'S THE CAPTAIN'S OWN BUSINESS, ISN'T IT?

OF COURSE, OF COURSE. I'M JUST... I'M SORRY.

BEING UNABLE TO COMMUNICATE WITH OUR SURVIVOR— IT MAKES ME TRY FOR SUCCESS IN OTHER AREAS, I SUPPOSE.

ACKNOWLEDGED, COMMANDER. LA FORGE **OUT**.

IF ONLY THERE WERE SOME WAY TO—TO **TURN OFF** HIS **GUILT** FOR A MOMENT. TO CLEAR AWAY THE CLUTTER FROM HIS **MIND**...

WAIT.

WHAT WAS THAT, COUNSELOR? WHAT DID YOU SAY?

JUST... TURN OFF HIS **GUILT** FOR A MOMENT. GEORDI, I KNOW IT SOUNDS **SILLY**, I WAS JUST—

NO, NO. THAT'S JUST **RIGHT**. I DON'T KNOW WHAT I WAS **THINKING**. I WAS SO FOCUSED ON LETTING **US** SEE **MORE**...

...THAT I IGNORED THE FACT THAT WHAT WE NEEDED WAS FOR **HIM** TO SEE **LESS**.

WHAT?

I CAN SET UP A *DAMPING* FIELD FROM *ENGINEERING* WHICH WOULD SUPPRESS THE ZOOR ENERGY ABOARD THE SHIP AND KEEP HIM FROM SEEING THESE GHOSTS...

...WHATEVER THEY ARE.

AND SO, IF YOU'RE RIGHT, COUNSELOR, THIS MAY LET HIM CONCENTRATE AND TALK TO YOU.

BUT GEORDI— HIS WOUNDS ARE KEPT IN CHECK BY THE ENERGY, TOO.

IF WE *SUPPRESS* IT—

OKAY, I *THINK* I CAN MODULATE THE LEVEL OF SUPPRESSION SO THAT WE CAN BLOCK OUT THE *GHOSTS* BUT KEEP HIM FROM *BLEEDING.*

I'LL GET RIGHT TO WORK ON IT.

GEORDI, THIS IS *FANTASTIC.*

THIS COULD BE THE *BREAKTHROUGH.*

ALL THAT REMAINS IS WHETHER *UUL EVERUUD* WILL TELL US WHAT HIS SHIP'S LOGS *CAN'T*—

"—AND HIS FELLOW COUNTRYMEN *WON'T.*"

AH!

COMMANDER RIKER, HOW GOOD OF YOU TO JOIN US!

ASTOUNDING, THAT TRANSPORTER TECHNOLOGY OF YOURS, COMMANDER.

IF ONLY JUULET HAD ACCESS TO SUCH A THING, IT WOULD—

DEERON!

WHAT THE HELL ARE YOU THINKING!?

C-COMMANDER?

AS IF IT WEREN'T ENOUGH THAT YOU MOVE UP YOUR SCHEDULE WITHOUT NOTIFYING US—

—OR THAT YOU BOARDED THE SHIP THREE HOURS EARLY—

—BUT TO HAVE ANOTHER EXPOSURE OF THE SAME ENERGY THAT CAUSED THE *FIRST* ACCIDENT...!!

YOU PEOPLE REALLY ARE BEYOND *BELIEF*. YOU WANT TO BE IN THE FEDERATION SO BADLY, AND TO HAVE ALL OF THE THINGS THAT MEMBERSHIP CAN PROVIDE...

...BUT YOU HAVE NO NOTION OF HOW TO CONDUCT YOURSELVES. CONTINUED UNSAFE PRACTICES, CONTEMPT FOR *INQUIRIES* INTO YOUR METHODS, AND LIES UPON *LIES*.

I'VE LOST MY PATIENCE WITH YOU, DEERON, AND YOUR COUNCIL. IT'S JUST—

COMMANDER, *PLEASE.*

ONE *MOMENT.*

WE ARE IN THE MIDST OF AN EXCEEDINGLY RARE ARMISTICE WITH THE DOROSSHIANS, WHOSE GENERAL PATTERN OF BEHAVIOR YOU YOURSELF HAVE WITNESSED.

RUDE, PRIMITIVE, MERCENARY, *SELFISH*.

ELDER KALKASS IS THE WORST OF THE COLLECTION OF WARLORDS; HE IS A STRONGHOLD IN THEIR OLD WAY OF THINKING—A WAY THAT EXPLOITS THE WEAK AND EMPOWERS THE STRONG.

YOU MUST KNOW OF THIS PHILOSOPHY, COMMANDER—

—IT WAS THE MILLSTONE AROUND YOUR SOCIETY'S NECK AS YOU ACHIEVED WARP CAPABILITY.

WERE YOU NOT STILL FIGHTING THOSE ELEMENTS ON YOUR WORLD WHEN YOU JOINED THE FEDERATION?

THAT HASN'T ANSWERED ANY OF MY—

BY NO MEANS ARE WE A PERFECT *CULTURE*, COMMANDER. THE STRUGGLE TO KEEP OUT THE CREEPING TENDRILS OF *CHAOS* LEADS ONE TO SOLUTIONS THAT OTHERS MAY FIND... UNPALATABLE.

DO WE *WISH* TO ORBIT THE PLANET AND SPY ON THE DOROSSHIANS?

NO.

WOULD WE PREFER TO TRUST THEM TO KEEP THEIR PROMISES?

CERTAINLY.

BUT ALLIOS IV IS POISED TO TAKE A GREAT *LEAP*, AND THE ARE *OUR* MILLSTONE, COMMANDER...

...KALKASS AND HIS CRONIES IN THE ELDER COUNCIL.

"THEIR?"

THERE'S ONLY *ONE* OF THEM LEFT, DEERON.

YES, WELL, OUR WORK HAS BEEN *SUCCESSFUL*, HASN'T IT?

HOLD IT. YOU'RE ADMITTING TO—?

I'M ADMITTING THAT THE ADVANCE OF OUR CIVILIZATION MEANS THAT THE GLORY DAYS OF THOSE WHO WOULD LIVE IN LUXURY AT THEIR PEOPLE'S EXPENSE IS DRAWING TO A CLOSE.

THEIR REWARDS WERE *WANING*.

MY GUESS IS THAT THEY HAVE TAKEN WHAT THEY COULD AND *LEFT*.

PRETTY THIN, THIS THEORY OF YOURS, DEERON.

NO *THINNER* THAN THAT WE HAVE SOMEHOW *OBLITERATED* THEM WITHOUT A *TRACE*, COMMANDER.

TOUCHE.

COMMANDER, *COME.* THIS MUTUAL ANTAGONISM IS TIRESOME.

MEET THE CREW, AND PLEASE, INSPECT OUR *REPAIRS.*

YES, WELL, IT *IS* QUITE A CREW YOU HAVE.

YES. OF COURSE, ONE HATES TO SHOW PREFERENTIAL TREATMENT...

...BUT FEMALES OF OUR SPECIES HAVE SUCH AN APTITUDE FOR *MECHANICS.*

AS FOR ME, I MERELY *SUPERVISE.* MY TECHNICAL KNOWLEDGE IS MINIMAL.

LEADERSHIP HAS ITS OWN CHALLENGES WITHOUT MIRING ONESELF IN *TECHNICALITIES,* DON'T YOU AGREE?

I AGREE ENTIRELY. I'M NOT TERRIBLY TECHNICAL MYSELF.

AH!

HERE'S WHAT YOU'RE HERE TO *SEE.*

THE *ZOOR LENSES.*

ALL RIGHT...

...OUR READINGS ON THE *ENTERPRISE* DETECTED WHAT SEEMS TO BE A HUGE OUTPUT OF THE SAME ENERGY THAT CAUSED THE FIRST EXPLOSION, DEERON.

CARE TO COMMENT ON THAT?

AH, YES.

WHEN WE CAME ABOARD, OUR TEMPORARY HOUSING FOR THE ZOOR ORE PIECES WERE APPROACHING THE END OF THEIR WINDOW OF USE, AND WE THOUGHT IT BEST TO PUT THEM INTO THE PERMANENT CASING HERE ON THE SHIP.

HMM.

THE DAMAGE TO THE CASING WAS SIMPLY A WORN-OUT SEAL AND *BOLT*.

AS YOU HAVE SEEN, OF COURSE, THE COST IN LIVES WAS *HIGHER*.

RIGHT, SO THE SPIKE IN *ENERGY...?*

UH, YES... THE BRIEF TRANSITION BETWEEN THE TWO SHIELDED COMPARTMENTS RELEASED SOME ENERGY.

OUR TECHNICIANS WHO WERE WITHIN THE RADIUS OF THE TRANSFER WERE WEARING SHIELDED SUITS, COMMANDER.

WE WON'T MAKE THE SAME MISTAKE TWICE.

-:SIGH:- ALL RIGHT, I HAVE TO SAY: YOUR EXPLANATIONS ARE VERY *THOROUGH*.

AND THE SUSPICIONS OF THE DOROSSHIANS—AND I'LL ADMIT, MINE AS WELL— SEEM TO BE BASED ONLY ON A LACK OF UNDERSTANDING.

BUT AFTER ALL THIS, WHY DO YOU HAVE THE ORE ABOARD?

WHY IS IT *HERE?*

OH, WELL, COMMANDER RIKER, ISN'T IT *OBVIOUS?*

POWER.

UH...

THIS SHIP DOESN'T OPERATE ITSELF, OF COURSE. AND THE MECHANISMS ABOARD NEED A PRIME MOVER TO DO ANYTHING AT ALL.

YES, COMMANDER.

POWER.

THE DISCOVERY OF THIS ORE DEEP IN THE CENTER OF OUR PLANET HAS *REVOLUTIONIZED* OUR CULTURE.

JUST TWENTY QUADS AGO WE WERE SCARCELY AHEAD OF THE *DOROSSHIANS*.

NOW WE ARE POISED TO ENTER THE *FEDERATION*.

THIS ORE HAS BEEN THE KEY TO SO MANY ADVANCEMENTS.

WITHOUT IT, WE WOULD BE NOTHING MORE THAN ONE MORE WARRING PLANET ON THE OUTER RIM.

IT'S AMAZING, COMMANDER, WHAT SUCH A SIMPLE THING LIKE *POWER* CAN DO FOR A PEOPLE—

"—IT LETS THEM SEE SOLUTIONS SO *CLEARLY*."

OKAY, GEORDI—A LITTLE MORE IS OKAY...

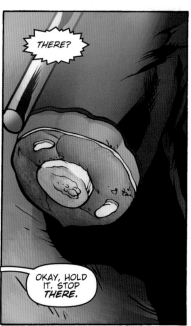

THERE?

OKAY, HOLD IT. STOP *THERE*.

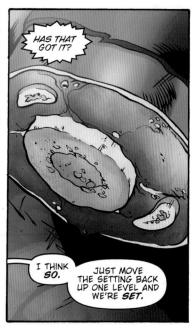

HAS THAT GOT IT?

I THINK *SO*.

JUST MOVE THE SETTING BACK UP ONE LEVEL AND WE'RE *SET*.

GREAT. I'LL BE DOWN THERE IN A FEW MINUTES.

EXCELLENT. THANKS, GEORDI. CRUSHER OUT.

SO, BEVERLY...

...DO YOU THINK IT WILL WORK?

IT SEEMS REASONABLE. THE *DISPLAY* SHOWS THAT THE ENERGY SCARCELY EXTENDS BEYOND HIS WOUNDS.

I THINK WHEN HE COMES OUT OF SEDATION, YOU SHOULD BE ABLE TO SPEAK WITH A FAR MORE LUCID PATIENT.

WELL, THAT WOULD BE *WONDERFUL*.

IT WILL MAKE EVERYTHING SO MUCH EASIER—AT LEAST FOR ME AND *HIM*.

FOR THE *CAPTAIN*, THOUGH— I JUST WISH HE'D COME DOWN HERE TO *TALK*.

HE'S SO CONCERNED ABOUT BEING A ROCK FOR THE CREW TO HOLD ON TO IN ALL THIS CONFUSION—

—THAT HE'S CUT HIMSELF *OFF* FROM THE PEOPLE HE WANTS TO *HELP*.

IF HE JUST WOULD HELP *HIMSELF* FIRST, HE...

...HE WOULD BE A FAR BETTER *CAPTAIN.*

CAPTAIN!

HELLO, COUNSELOR.

BEVERLY, HAVE I ARRIVED IN *TIME?*

JUST.

AND JEAN-LUC...

...GOOD TO SEE YOU.

BEE BEEP

UNNH...

UUL? UUL, CAN YOU HEAR ME?

RESEARCHER EVERUUD?

NNH...

WH... WHERE AM I..

YOU'RE ABOARD THE FEDERATION STARSHIP *ENTERPRISE.*

I'M—

F-FEDERATION, HUH? K-KEJAAL AND DEERON S-SHOULD BE PLEASED...

ER... YES.

NOW, RESEARCHER *EVERUUD*, CAN YOU SEE THE GHOSTS THAT WERE SURROUNDING YOU BEFORE?

N-NO, I CAN'T. TH-THEY'RE *GONE*. I—

I CAN'T BELIEVE IT. THEY'RE—

OH, NO, WAIT. THERE'S ONE.

OH, NO, NO, RESEARCHER EVERUUD—

THIS IS OUR *CAPTAIN*, AND HE'S VERY MUCH *ALIVE*.

HOW DO YOU DO. I AM JEAN-LUC PICARD, THE CAPTAIN OF THIS STARSHIP.

I'M GLAD WE CAN FINALLY *TALK*.

SO LET US TALK ABOUT YOUR *GHOSTS*.

NHH... I'M SO *TIRED*...

...THEY JUST TALKED AND TALKED TO ME, TELLING ME *SECRETS*... NUMBERS...

"NUMBERS?"

BUT WHO *WERE* THEY, UUL? AND WHY WAS OUR *CAPTAIN* ONE OF THEM?

THAT LEADER—ELDER WITH THE ANGRY *HEIR*—

WHAT—? *KALKASS* IS ONE OF YOUR GHOSTS?

Y-YES. KALKASS.

MM.

ONE MOMENT.

PICARD TO WORF. IS ELDER KALKASS WITH YOU?

NO, CAPTAIN. HE BECAME UPSET AND LEFT US. THEN WORIKK INSULTED ME SO I HAVE BEEN FINISHING MY RESEARCH IN AN EMPTY BUILDING.

AN INSULT? AH... I HOPE YOU WERE ABLE TO TAKE APPROPRIATE STEPS...?

YES, SIR.

ABSOLUTELY.

LIEUTENANT, I NEED YOU TO LOCATE ELDER KALKASS IMMEDIATELY.

I BELIEVE HE MAY BE IN *DANGER*.

YES, SIR, RIGHT AWAY. I'LL REPORT IN AS SOON AS I *FIND* HIM.

WORF *OUT*.

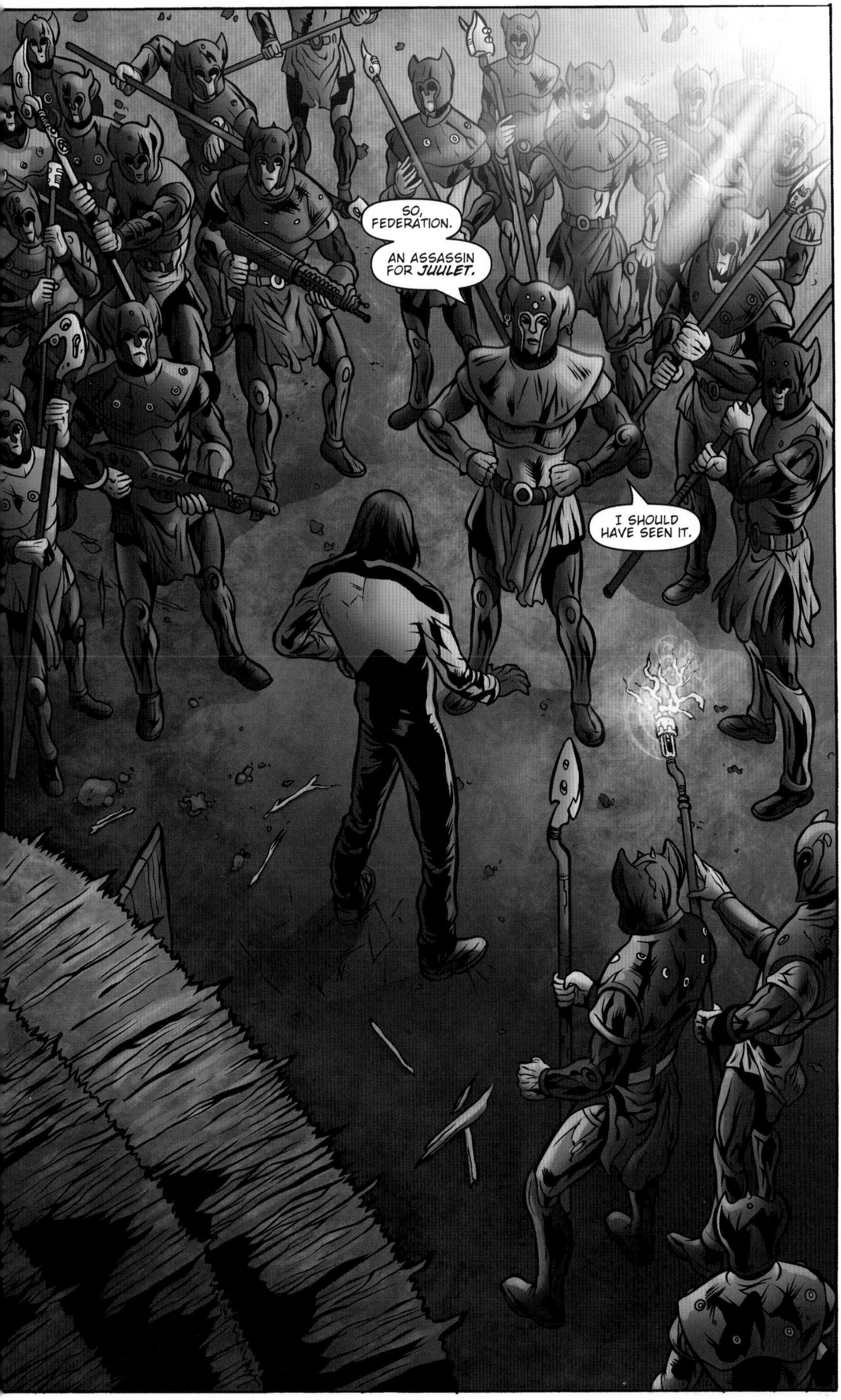
SO, FEDERATION.
AN ASSASSIN FOR JUULET.
I SHOULD HAVE SEEN IT.

WHAT—? YOU ARE MISTAKEN, WORIKK. I HAVE KILLED NO ONE.

AH, BUT DON'T YOUR MASTERS SAY THERE IS NO WEAPON IN THE SKY? THERE IS NO SIGN OF MY FATHER—

—SAVE FOR HIS BOOT—

—AND DO YOU NOT HAVE, FEDERATION—

HEY!

—A WEAPON THAT VAPORIZES ITS TARGET, LEAVING NO TRACE?

WORIKK, I HAVE DONE NOTHING TO YOUR FATHER.

FEDERATION ASSASSIN—BY OUR ELDER LAWS... ...YOU ARE OUR PRISONER. YOU WILL COME WITH US.

WORF TO ENTERPRISE. ONE TO BEAM—

HUH. WHAT'S THE MATTER, FEDERATION? DO YOU RUN AWAY FROM A FIGHT TO RETURN TO YOUR "WARRIOR CULTURE?"

NO, IT WAS JUST HALF A MESSAGE, CAPTAIN.

HE STOPPED IN THE MIDDLE OF HIS SENTENCE.

ALL RIGHT, MR. O'BRIEN. GET HIM OUT OF THERE.

SIR, HIS COMMBADGE, IT'S COME OFF.

JUST HONE IN AND BEAM HIM UP, O'BRIEN.

SIR—THERE'RE DOZENS OF THEM, ALL OVER.

I CAN'T TELL WHICH ONE IS *WORF!*

EVERYONE'S *MOVING*—WE'VE GOT *INJURIES*—

ONE'S VITALS AT HALF-STRENGTH—

GET HIM *OUT* OF THERE, O'BRIEN!

SIR, I'M *TRYING*—I CAN'T LOCK ON TO *ANYONE!*

I CAN'T TELL WHO'S WHO!

ALL STATIONS—

—RED ALERT.

ᴿᴿᵀᴱᴿᴿᵀᴱᴿᴿᵀᴱᴿᴿᵀᴱᴿᴿᵀᴱᴿᴿᵀᴱᴿᴿᵀ

ENSIGN, CAN YOU CONFIRM WHAT CHIEF O'BRIEN IS SEEING?

YES, SIR— A HUGE MOB— HUNDREDS NOW.

WHAT'S *HAPPENING?*

O'BRIEN SAYS WORF'S LOST HIS COMMBADGE— WHERE *IS* HE—!

NUMBER ONE— I NEED YOU TO TAKE A SECURITY DETAIL AND—

SIR, WE'RE BEING *HAILED.*

ON SCREEN!

SKKKTAIN PICARD, I CAN ONLY BLAME MYSELF FOR MY NAIVETE—

—YOU SPEAK AS THE GIRLISH JUULETIANS DO—

—AND YOU SEND US A FALSE WARRIOR TO **KILL** FOR THEM.

IN HINDSIGHT IT'S **OBVIOUS**, FEDERATION.

HOW FOOLISH OF ME—AND MY LATE FATHER—NOT TO SEE IT.

YOU ARE **WRONG**, WORIKK.

WE ARE EMISSARIES OF **PEACE**.

OUR CULTURE DESIRES NOTHING BUT TO PROMOTE UNDERSTANDING THROUGHOUT—

I HAVE KKK HEARD THOSE WORDS **BEFORE**, FEDERATION.

FROM OUR ASSASSIN **NEIGHBORS**.

WE ARE FINISHED WITH SIMPLY LISTENING TO THEIR BLEATING ABOUT **JUSTICE**—

—AND PREPARED TO BEGIN DISPENSING OUR OWN.

YOU WILL MOVE ALL OF YOUR GUNSHIPS FROM OUR SKY—YOU WILL DELIVER US THEIR LEADERS TO BE JUDGED—

—OR YOUR WEAK LITTLE **WARRIOR**—

—WILL **DIE** FOR THEM.

Chapter 3

WELL, SPEAKER KEJAAL...

...YOU WERE NOT LYING ABOUT THE SIZE OF YOUR COUNTRY'S ARCHIVES.

INDEED, COMMANDER DATA...

...WE'RE QUITE PROUD THAT OUR LIBRARY IS THE MOST COMPLETE—

NO.

I MEAN THAT *HONESTY* IS A KEY FACTOR IN CONSIDERATION FOR FEDERATION MEMBERSHIP.

OH, UH...

~AHEM~

YES, OF *COURSE.*

MY REPORT ON YOUR COUNTRY IS NEARLY COMPLETE. THANK YOU, SPEAKER KEJAAL, FOR ALL YOUR ASSISTANCE.

I HOPE MY COLLEAGUE, LIEUTENANT *WORF,* FINDS YOUR NEIGHBORS THE *DOROSSHIANS* AS COOPERATIVE.

YES, WELL...

...I'M NOT CERTAIN HE *WILL.* OUR FEUD HAS—

ENTERPRISE TO *DATA.*

EXCUSE ME, SPEAKER KEJAAL. YES, DATA HERE.

COMMANDER, PREPARE TO BEAM UP. THERE HAS BEEN AN EMERGENCY THAT NEEDS YOUR ATTENTION.

RIGHT AWAY, CHIEF O'BRIEN.

AND, DATA, IS SPEAKER KEJAAL WITH YOU?

YES.

THE CAPTAIN'S ASKED THAT I BEAM *HIM* UP AS WELL—

"—THERE'S SOMETHING HE OUGHT TO *SEE.*"

CAPTAIN'S LOG, STARDATE 44751.5.

I HAVE BROUGHT THE LEADERS OF THE *REPUBLIC OF JUULET* ABOARD THE *ENTERPRISE* TO SHOW THEM THE ENDS TO WHICH THEIR CONSTANT WARRING WITH THEIR NEIGHBOR, THE *NATION OF DOROSSH*, HAS LED.

LIEUTENANT WORF, WHILE ON A FACT-FINDING MISSION IN DOROSSH, WAS ACCUSED OF MURDERING THE SOLE REMAINING *ELDER* OF THEIR GOVERNMENT.

THE NEW REGIME, LED BY THE LAST ELDER'S HEIR, WORIKK, HAS ARRESTED WORF AND TAKEN HIM TO A SECRET LOCATION, WHERE THEY SAY HE WILL BE EXECUTED UNLESS THEIR DEMANDS ARE MET.

WH—WHAT ARE THEIR *DEMANDS?*

THEY'VE DEMANDED THAT WE MOVE YOUR SURVEILLANCE SHIP OUT OF THE GEOSYNCHRONOUS ORBIT ABOVE THEIR NATION, AND—

WELL, CERTAINLY. LET'S GET STARTED RIGHT *AWAY*, CAPTAIN.

ABSOLUTELY *NOT*. THE FEDERATION DOES NOT ACCEDE TO THE DEMANDS OF *TERRORISTS*, NOT EVEN IF—

OH, BUT CAPTAIN, *PLEASE*...

...YOUR OFFICER'S *LIFE* IS IN *DANGER*— WE *MUST* MOVE IT.

I UNDERSTAND YOUR UNWILLINGNESS TO SET A PRECEDENT, BUT...

...YOUR OFFICER'S *PRESENCE* THERE IS AN *ANOMALY* TO BEGIN WITH. ONCE HE'S *RETURNED*, I CAN ASSURE YOU, NO JUULETIAN WILL PUT HIMSELF IN THAT POSITION.

JUST THIS ONCE, CAPTAIN, WE MAY GIVE IN TO THEIR DEMANDS.

YOU MAKE A PASSIONATE ARGUMENT, SPEAKER KEJAAL.

THEN IT IS *SETTLED*. WHAT ARE THEIR OTHER DEMANDS?

JUST *ONE*. THAT WE TURN YOU BOTH *OVER* TO THEM.

UH, WAIT, WAIT, WAIT...

RELAX, SPEAKER KEJAAL.

AS THE CAPTAIN SAID, THE FEDERATION WILL NOT GIVE IN TO RANSOMS OR TO DEMANDS MADE BY THOSE WHO THREATEN US.

YOU'RE *SAFE* WITH US.

BUT WE DO NEED TO GET OUR OFFICER BACK.

THAT'S WHERE YOU COME IN.

YOU *KNOW* THE DOROSSHIAN CULTURE.

THERE ARE NEARLY A *MILLION* INDIVIDUALS IN DOROSSH'S CAPITAL, WITHIN A KILOMETER OF WHERE WORF WAS ARRESTED.

WHERE CAN HE HAVE BEEN *TAKEN*? I MEAN—

"—HE CAN'T HAVE JUST VANISHED INTO THIN AIR."

KL'K'AK

YOU MAY GO, COLOXX.

I WISH TO SPEAK TO THE PRISONER *ALONE.*

HAH.

SO, FEDERATION...

...HAVE YOU GIVEN UP *ALREADY?*

HERE WE PROVIDE YOU A *CHAIR* YET YOU KNEEL ON THE FLOOR IN *DEFERENCE.*

OH, WOULDN'T YOUR *"WARRIOR ANCESTORS"* BE ASHAMED?

IT IS NOT *YOU* TO WHOM I KNEEL, WORIKK.

NO?

YOU HAD *BETTER,* FEDERATION. MY DEAD FATHER CALLS FOR *JUSTICE...*

...AND MY MERCY MAY BE ALL THAT SAVES YOUR NECK FROM THE *AXE.*

YOUR SOCIETY IS *ANYTHING* BUT *JUST,* WORIKK.

IF THE ONLY WAY FOR ME TO LIVE IS TO PLEAD FOR YOU TO *SPARE* ME...

...THEN I WILL *DIE.*

SO IT IS NOT *YOU* I KNEEL TO...

...BUT MY *WARRIOR ANCESTORS* AND MY *WARRIOR GOD.*

TO PLEAD WITH THEM TO SEE THE HONOR IN MY DEATH—

—DESPITE THE FACT THAT I AM SOON TO DIE BY YOUR *TREACHERY.*

WHAT?

YOU ARE NOT THE SIMPLE BARBARIAN YOU PRETEND TO BE.

YOU KNOW VERY WELL I DID NOT KILL YOUR FATHER.

BUT IT WAS SIMPLE TO PLAY ON YOUR PEOPLE'S IGNORANCE IN ORDER TO GET YOURSELF A BARGAINING CHIP.

HM.

I *DISAGREE,* MURDERER.

BUT IF THE FEDERATION SEES FIT TO SEND OVER THOSE WHO ORDERED MY FATHER'S DEATH—

—THEN I SHALL SEE FIT TO RETURN THEIR *ERRAND BOY.*

PERHAPS YOU SHOULD PRAY YOUR CAPTAIN EVEN *WANTS* YOU BACK...

"...WHEN HE SEES WHAT YOU'VE BEEN REDUCED TO."

NNH...

QUITE A LONG SLEEP YOU HAD.

I BET *THAT* CLEARED AWAY SOME COBWEBS.

HOW ARE YOU FEELING?

OHH...

I-I'M FEELING FINE, I GUESS. B-BUT WHAT *HAPPENED* TO ME?

OH—OH, BY THE *CORE*—WHERE'S MY *HAND*—WHERE'S MY *LEG*?!

RESEARCHER EVERUUD, I'M SORRY, YOU APPEAR TO HAVE BEEN INJURED IN AN *EXPLOSION.*

A VERY *STRANGE* EXPLOSION...

...BECAUSE WHILE IT SEEMS TO HAVE VAPORIZED YOUR CREWMATES, THE SURVEILLANCE SHIP ITSELF IS UNTOUCHED.

OHH, I FEEL SICK— I DON'T—

A-AND— WHAT SURVEILLANCE SHIP? M-MY CREW AND I WERE ON A MILITARY MISSION TO—

AH! SO HERE IS OUR LONG-LOST LOYAL COMRADE!

FINALLY WE CAN SEE OUR BRAVE SURVIVOR!

YOU HAVE A **MEDAL** COMING TO YOU, UUL. FORTITUDE IN THE FACE OF EXTREME PERIL!

BEVERLY—HIS **FEAR** RESPONSE...!

I SEE IT TOO, DEANNA—THE READINGS ON THE INSTRUMENTS JUST JUMPED OFF THE CHARTS!

H-HELLO, SPEAKER KEJAAL. D-DEERON.

HELLO, DR. CRUSHER, COUNSELOR TROI.

GOOD TO SEE YOU IN SUCH CAPABLE HANDS, UUL.

WE'VE ONLY HEARD BITS ABOUT HOW YOU WERE DOING...

...SOMETHING ABOUT **GHOSTS** HAUNTING YOU?

UNSETTLING. PARTICULARLY FOR SOMEONE SO SCIENTIFIC.

ER, Y-YES, VERY UNSETTLING.

NOW, DR. CRUSHER, MAY WE EXPECT RESEARCHER EVERUUD BACK DOWN PLANET-SIDE ANYTIME SOON? HIS FAMILY DEARLY WISHES TO SEE HIM.

WELL, WE DON'T RECOMMEND HE BE MOVED FOR SOME **TIME.**

HIS WOUNDS ARE **EXTENSIVE,** AND WE'VE ONLY JUST RECENTLY GOTTEN A SUPPRESSION FIELD IN PLACE TO FILTER OUT THE **ZOOR ENERGY,** AND THE GHOSTS, SO HE CAN SPEAK WITH US.

WE CERTAINLY DON'T WANT TO KEEP HIM FROM HIS FAMILY, BUT—

WELL, YES, **EXTENDED** FAMILY. AUNTS, UNCLES. NO SPOUSE, NO CHILDREN.

HE HASN'T TOLD YOU HE'S A BACHELOR? **SURPRISING.**

TWO PRETTY GIRLS LIKE YOU, I WOULD HAVE THOUGHT HE'D BRING IT **UP.**

UH, WELL, NO. ANYWAY, WE SHOULD CARRY ON. WE WILL HAVE THE CAPTAIN CONTACT YOU WHEN WE KNOW MORE ABOUT WHEN HE CAN GO HOME.

SO, IF YOU'LL EXCUSE US...

OF COURSE. JUST A FINAL, TRADITIONAL *SEND OFF.* DEERON?

YES, SIR. TAKE MY *HAND,* UUL.

CITIZEN, O CITIZEN, GREAT HAS BEEN YOUR SERVICE TO THE REPUBLIC. SHOULD YOU FALL, OR SHOULD YOU BE RESTORED FULLY TO US, YOU WILL HAVE THIS HONOR.

YOU HAVE *SUFFERED.* YOU FIND IT DIFFICULT TO *SPEAK.* YOU FIND IT DIFFICULT TO *SEE.*

YOU FIND IT DIFFICULT TO *REMEMBER.* YOU FIND IT DIFFICULT TO *UNDERSTAND.* THESE ARE ALL WOUNDS YOU HAVE SUFFERED IN OUR *NAME.*

BUT ON THE DAY WHEN ALL ARE ONE, THESE WOUNDS ARE TAKEN AWAY, AND THERE WILL BE NO SUFFERING.

TWO PATHS LEAD THERE.

MAY WE ALL TAKE THE CORRECT ONE.

FAREWELL, CITIZEN, O CITIZEN.

THANK YOU, DR. CRUSHER. COUNSELOR TROI.

GOOD TO SEE OUR RESEARCHER IN SUCH GOOD CARE.

STRANGE.

SO... ...UUL, YOU WERE *SAYING,* SOMETHING ABOUT A MILITARY MISSION...

...UH, *UUL?*

HELLO?

UUL? CAN YOU *HEAR* ME?

MR. DATA.

HAVE YOU FINISHED ENTERING THE SEARCH PARAMETERS THE JUULETIANS GAVE US?

YES, SIR.

THE INFORMATION WAS NOT SIGNIFICANTLY HELPFUL ABOVE WHAT WE HAD ALREADY DEDUCED, HOWEVER.

SPEAKER KEJAAL SUGGESTED WE LOOK FOR LIFE-FORMS THAT DO NOT MOVE OUT OF A PRESCRIBED SPACE, AND DEERON OFFERED THAT WE TRY LOOKING FOR A GROUP THAT ALL MOVE TOGETHER...

...BOTH OF WHICH WE HAD ALREADY ENTERED.

THEY WERE HELPFUL, SIR, AND THEIR IDEAS WERE SOUND, BUT THEY DIDN'T SHOW ANY SPECIAL KNOWLEDGE OF THE DOROSSHIANS OR THEIR CULTURE.

STRANGE FOR A COUNTRY WITH A MUCH-DISCUSSED SURVEILLANCE SHIP ABOVE DOROSSH.

WHAT'S THE STATUS OF THE SEARCH NOW, DATA?

PROGRESSING, COMMANDER. CURRENTLY THE NUMBER OF HITS THAT MATCH ALL OF OUR CRITERIA IS 361,948 AND DROPPING.

THEY'RE DROPPING FAR TOO SLOWLY FOR MY TASTE.

WHAT ABOUT KLINGON BIOSIGNS? SURELY HE'S THE ONLY ONE DOWN THERE.

HE IS, SIR...

...BUT SCANNING TO THE DEPTH THAT WOULD DIFFERENTIATE HIM TAKES 91.44 SECONDS PER INDIVIDUAL.

WE'RE RUNNING IT CONSTANTLY BUT WITH THE HIGH VOLUME OF INDIVIDUALS, IT WILL TAKE—

—MORE TIME THAN WE'VE GOT. OKAY.

CAPTAIN, THE SEARCHES ARE ALL RUNNING AT TOP SPEED. I WILL NOTIFY YOU OF OUR PROGRESS AS WE NARROW DOWN OUR OPTIONS.

THANK YOU, DATA. CARRY ON.

WELL, DATA... ...I HAVE TO SAY, THE AMOUNT OF INFORMATION YOU'VE PUT INTO YOUR REPORT ON JUULET IS AMAZING.

THANK YOU, SIR.

HISTORIES, CULTURAL NORMS, PROGRESSION OF LANGUAGE, HAND PHYSIOLOGY, NUMBER SYSTEMS...

IT WILL TAKE A WHILE TO GET THROUGH, BUT IT WILL BE OF GREAT USE TO US ON THE BRIDGE.

THANK YOU.

I AM, HOWEVER, CONCERNED ABOUT ONE SECTION THAT IS INCOMPLETE.

REALLY? WHICH ONE?

WELL, SIR, THE DISCOVERY AND HARNESSING OF THE ORE FROM THEIR PLANET'S CENTER—THE ONE THAT PRODUCES *ZOOR ENERGY*—SEEMS TO BE THE DRIVING FORCE BEHIND THE JUULETIAN SOCIETY'S ADVANCEMENT...

...AND YET I WAS UNABLE TO FIND EVEN THE *SMALLEST* PIECE OF SCIENTIFIC DATA ON THE ORE *ITSELF*.

THROUGH MY STUDY OF THE COUNTRY'S *HISTORY*, I HAVE IDENTIFIED A NUMBER OF INDIVIDUALS WHO MADE DISCOVERIES OR ADVANCES IN THE FIELD.

CROSS-REFERENCING THAT INFORMATION WITH RAW DATA OF RESIDENTIAL AND WORK ADDRESSES, I HAVE FOUND *THIS*.

COORDINATES. OKAY, SO WHAT DO YOU THINK IS *HERE*?

THIS IS THE LOCATION THAT SAW THE MOST SIGNIFICANT ADVANCES IN HARNESSING THE PROPERTIES OF THE ORE.

IT'S AN ENTIRE FLOOR OF ONE OF THEIR HIGHEST BUILDINGS. I WAS DENIED ACCESS, THOUGH THEY DID NOT SUSPECT I KNEW ITS IMPORTANCE.

IN ANY CASE, SIR, I THOUGHT I'D BRING IT TO YOUR ATTENTION.

IT'S VERY LIKELY THIS LOCATION CONTAINS SOME KEY INSIGHT INTO THE NATURE OF THIS *ZOOR ORE*.

ITS *NATURE*?

DEERON TOLD ME IT'S A *POWER SOURCE* FOR THE SHIP.

I DON'T SEE WHY—

I'M SORRY, SIR, BUT I'M AFRAID YOU HAVE BEEN *MISINFORMED*.

WHAT?

ACCORDING TO LT. COMMANDER LA FORGE, THE JUULETIAN SHIP IS POWERED BY A MATTER/ANTIMATTER REACTION ASSEMBLY SIMILAR TO OURS.

IN FACT, SIR...

...ENERGY IS RELEASED *INTO* THE ORE CHAMBER ON THE JUULETIAN SHIP.

THE LIKELIHOOD IS THAT THE SHIP *IS* A WEAPON... ...JUST AS DOROSSH HAS SAID.

DAMN IT. I THOUGHT WE WERE ALL *LEVELING* WITH EACH OTHER, BUT—

—MORE *LIES.* I DON'T *KNOW.*

AND WHAT DOES IT *MATTER,* WITH WORF CAPTURED?

WHAT DOES IT MATTER TO *HIM* WHAT THE SURVEILLANCE SHIP DOES?

WE SHOULD SEND SOMEONE DOWN TO *FIND* HIM, NOT WORRY ABOUT THIS CIVIL *WAR.*

PERHAPS, COMMANDER...

...BUT IF WE *PROVE* THAT THE SHIP DID KILL ELDER KALKASS—

—BY EXAMING THE RESEARCH SITE AT THESE COORDINATES—

—THE DOROSSHIANS WOULD *HAVE* TO SET LT. WORF FREE.

I DON'T KNOW, DATA. I DOUBT THE DOROSSHIANS EVER FEEL THAT THEY *HAVE* TO DO ANYTHING.

FROM WHAT I'VE SEEN, THEY'RE LITTLE MORE THAN—

MR. DATA, COMMANDER— DOROSSH IS *HAILING* US.

ON SCREEN.

SKKKAPTAIN PICARD, ARE YOU A *DEAD MAN?* ARE YOU A *GHOST?*

YOU FLOAT, SILENT, IN THE SKY, DOING *NOTHING.*

YOU HAVE NOT MOVED THE GUN-SHIP, CAPTAIN. YOU HAVE NOT GIVEN US THE JUULETIAN LEADERS.

AND WE *SHALL* NOT, WORIKK. AS I TOLD YOU, THE FEDERATION AND THE *ENTERPRISE* DO NOT RESPOND TO *THREATS.*

VERY WELL.

YOU TOY WITH YOUR ASSASSIN'S LIFE, CAPTAIN.

WITH EVERY MOMENT YOU SIT THERE, STALLING, TERRIFIED TO MAKE A DECISION, YOUR "WARRIOR" TAKES THE LAST FEW STEPS INTO HIS *GRAVE.*

AND WHAT ASSURANCE DO I HAVE THAT HE IS NOT DEAD *ALREADY?*

HAH. WARRIORS OF DOROSSH! LET OUR ENEMIES SEE THEIR FAILED KILLER!

LET THEM SEE WHAT HE IS NOW!

HA HA HA HA HA

HERE HE IS, CAPTAIN.

REDUCED TO...

...A SHADOW.

IS WHAT YOU SEE BEFORE YOU STILL WHAT YOU CALL A *WARRIOR?*

WORIKK, I SEE A WARRIOR WHO HAS FOUGHT AGAINST IMPOSSIBLE ODDS.

I SEE A WARRIOR WHO HAS HAD HIS STRENGTH *STRIPPED* FROM HIM.

I SEE A WARRIOR OF GREAT VIRTUE WHO FEARS IF HE IS EXECUTED THAT HE WILL NOT BE FOUND WORTHY IN HIS FINAL JUDGMENT.

BUT HE SHOULD KNOW:

IF IT TAKES EVERYTHING THIS CREW AND THIS SHIP HAS TO GIVE, AND ALL THE TIME ANY OF US HAS LEFT—

—HE WILL ENTER HIS WARRIOR HEAVEN.

BAH! PRETTY WORDS FROM THE WEAK AND TREACHEROUS.

THEY SIGNIFY ABSOLUTELY NOTH—

...WISHES TO DWELL IN A WARRIOR HEAVEN...

...WARRIOR...

...STOVOKOR...

...HIS DEDICATION...

COULD HE BE...

WHAT ARE YOU FOOLS TALKING ABOUT?

WORIKK—YOUR WARS AGAINST JUULET HAVE BEEN LONG AND HARD-FOUGHT. THERE IS MUCH CAUSE FOR COMPLAINT ON **BOTH** SIDES.

BUT LIEUTENANT WORF IS **BLAMELESS.**

WE DO NOT KNOW WHO, IF ANYONE, KILLED YOUR FATHER. AND THE PUNISHMENT OF THE INNOCENT, WORIKK—

—IT WILL NOT **STAND.**

YOUR DEMANDS WILL **NOT** BE MET. YOUR BULLYING WILL **NOT** BE REWARDED. YOU WILL NOT—

BAH.

TKKT

THESE FOOLS...

...AND THEIR LIES...

THEY...

...THEY WILL SEE...

THEY WILL SEE WHEN THEIR OFFICER LIES DEAD...

...THEY SHOULD NOT UNDERESTIMATE US.

YOU HEAR, MURDERER? YOUR CAPTAIN HAS SIGNED YOUR DEATH WARRANT!

THANK YOU, MY CAPTAIN.

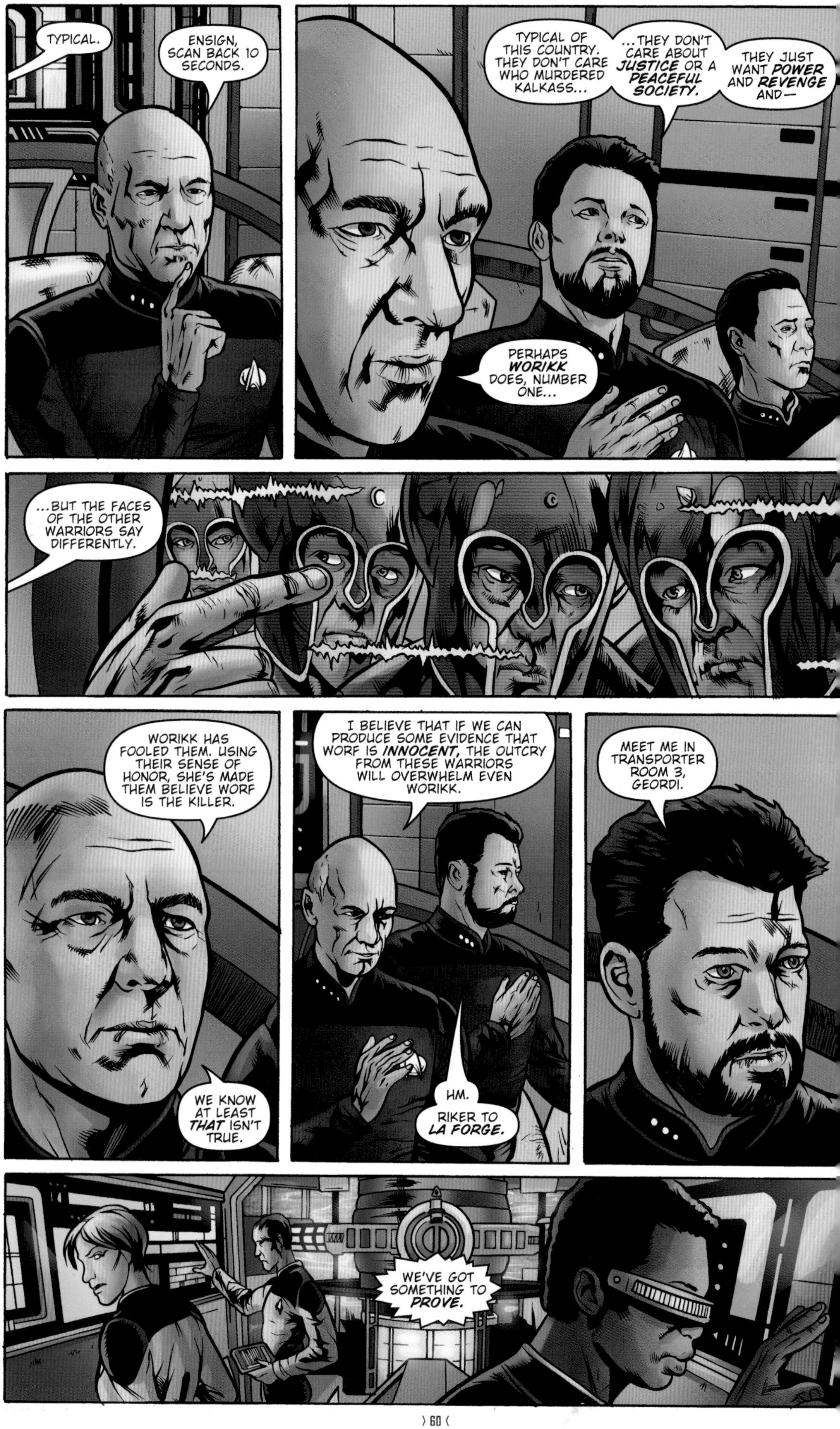
TYPICAL.
ENSIGN, SCAN BACK 10 SECONDS.
TYPICAL OF THIS COUNTRY. THEY DON'T CARE WHO MURDERED KALKASS...
...THEY DON'T CARE ABOUT JUSTICE OR A PEACEFUL SOCIETY.
THEY JUST WANT POWER AND REVENGE AND—
PERHAPS WORIKK DOES, NUMBER ONE...
...BUT THE FACES OF THE OTHER WARRIORS SAY DIFFERENTLY.
WORIKK HAS FOOLED THEM. USING THEIR SENSE OF HONOR, SHE'S MADE THEM BELIEVE WORF IS THE KILLER.
WE KNOW AT LEAST THAT ISN'T TRUE.
I BELIEVE THAT IF WE CAN PRODUCE SOME EVIDENCE THAT WORF IS INNOCENT, THE OUTCRY FROM THESE WARRIORS WILL OVERWHELM EVEN WORIKK.
HM.
RIKER TO LA FORGE.
MEET ME IN TRANSPORTER ROOM 3, GEORDI.
WE'VE GOT SOMETHING TO PROVE.

OKAY, UUL, YOU'VE ALREADY STATED THAT TWO OF THE GHOSTS YOU'VE SEEN WERE CAPTAIN PICARD AND ELDER KALKASS OF DOROSSH.

NOW, WHO ELSE? WHO ELSE HAUNTS YOU?

-:SIGH:-

COME ON, UUL. THIS *SILENCE* ISN'T HELPING. WHY WON'T YOU TALK TO US?

WE'RE TRYING TO *HELP* YOU.

UUL, IF YOU FEEL LIKE SAYING SOMETHING WOULD PUT YOUR LIFE IN DANGER, THE FEDERATION CAN *PROTECT* YOU.

WE NEED TO GET SOME ANSWERS... IN ORDER TO HELP BOTH YOU *AND* THE GHOSTS.

BEVERLY—

—HAVE YOU SEEN HOW EXTENSIVE DATA'S REPORT ON JUULET IS? SO MANY *TOPICS*—SO *COMPLETE*.

UH...

...NO, SORRY DEANNA, *I* HAVEN'T.

THIS IS *IMPORTANT.* CAPTAIN PICARD COULD BE AT RISK HERE, BUT UUL WON'T GIVE ANY MORE *INFORMATION.*

WE'VE TAKEN AWAY THE GHOSTS' VOICES THAT WERE DISTRACTING HIM...

...BUT NOW IT'S *FEAR* THAT'S KEEPING HIM QUIET.

UUL, IF YOU WOULD JUST TELL US WHO THESE GHOSTS *ARE*, WE COULD—

OH, YOU SHOULD SEE THIS, TOO, UUL. WHAT AN AMAZING COUNTRY YOU HAVE. ALL THE *ARCHITECTURE.* ALL THE *SCIENCE.*

ALL THE *PEOPLE.*

KEER EVERUUD.

KNOWN RELATIVES: *UUL EVERUUD,* HUSBAND.

VOCATION: GEOLOGIC RESEARCHER. ACCOMPLISHMENTS: REFINED ORE OUTPUT INTO DIRECTIONAL ENERGY STREAMS; RECIPIENT OF MUUR JUUSTAT PRIZE FOR PHYSICS.

CAUSE OF DEATH: UNKNOWN.

SO, UUL—WE THOUGHT YOU WERE A *BACHELOR.*

~HH~

WH—WHY ARE YOU D-DOING THIS? WHY ARE YOU TORTURING ME WITH HER *FACE?*

WHY C-CAN'T YOU JUST LET ME *FORGET?*

SHE'S ONE OF YOUR GHOSTS, ISN'T SHE, UUL? A LITTLE ACCIDENT WITH THE ORE YEARS AGO...

...AND NOW SHE'S *HERE,* TALKING TO YOU. *HAUNTING* YOU. BUT THIS ISN'T *GUILT,* UUL...

...IT'S *REAL.* SHE'S REAL. SHE'S TRAPPED. AND IF YOU *TALK* TO US, YOU CAN *HELP* HER.

MAYBE EVEN BRING HER *BACK.*

PLEASE, UUL—TELL US HER *STORY.*

"W-WE MET AT THE ORE RESEARCH CENTER UP IN THE GOVERNMENT BUILDING.

"PEOPLE BEFORE US HAD DISCOVERED THE ORE HAD PECULIAR PROPERTIES— WE WERE MEANT TO HARNESS THEM.

"OUR DISCOVERIES CAME FAST, AND WERE WELL RECEIVED. EVERY DAY WE FOUND NEW USES FOR THE ORE."

OKAY, GEORDI—

—LET'S BYPASS THE LOCK AND GET IN THERE.

"EVEN OUR FIRST *DISASTER* WAS LUCKY. NO ONE WAS INJURED WHEN I SPLIT A CHUNK OF ORE AND RELEASED A MASSIVE AMOUNT OF ZOOR ENERGY.

"IT SEEMED THAT WE—AND OUR LAB—WERE BLESSED. WE MADE DISCOVERY AFTER DISCOVERY—"

ALMOST GOT IT, COMMANDER.

"—AND THE LAB ITSELF WAS A REPOSITORY OF OUR NATION'S MOST VALUABLE SCIENTIFIC SECRETS."

WHAT...?

I DON'T GET IT. THESE ARE DATA'S EXACT COORDINATES. THERE'S NOTHING *HERE.*

"BUT THEN KEER DIED.

THEN I KILLED HER. WE HAD FOUND ONE MORE PROPERTY OF THE ORE.

DAMN IT. *ENTERPRISE.* TWO TO BEAM UP.

"THE ENERGY I HAD RELEASED IN THE ACCIDENT DIDN'T DISSIPATE AS I THOUGHT. IT DISAPPEARED, BUT..."

"WHEN KEER WAS WORKING LATE ONE NIGHT, AS I HAD BEEN...

"...AT THE SAME TIME OF NIGHT THAT I HAD MADE MY ERROR...

"...SOMETHING SWEPT THROUGH...

EEEEEEEEEEE

"...AND SHE WAS GONE.

WE CALLED IT "ORE PROPERTY 671: CORE-RELATIVE PERSISTENCE."

THEY WANTED TO NAME IT AFTER KEER, BUT I WOULDN'T LET THEM...

WAIT— —SO THE ENERGY *ORBITS* THE PLANET? IT JUST KEEPS COMING AROUND AT THE SAME HEIGHT AS WHERE IT WAS RELEASED?

NO, NO.

WE ORBIT THE PLANET. THE PLANET TURNS, AND WE TURN WITH IT. THE ENERGY JUST *STAYS*. SAME HEIGHT, SAME BEARING FROM THE CORE.

MAKING THAT EXACT RING AROUND THE PLANET *UNLIVABLE*.

IT'S LIKE THE CORE IS PUNISHING US FOR TAKING PART OF IT AWAY.

ITS ENERGY JUST *STAYS*, LURKING.

IT KILLED MY WIFE...

...IT KILLED MY CREW...

"...NOW IT'LL KILL ME."

COME.

BEE BOOP

CAPTAIN.

THERE IS NOTHING AT THE SITE THAT DATA GAVE US. WE WERE UNABLE TO UNCOVER ANY EVIDENCE TO HELP WORF.

RECOMMEND WE SEND AN AWAY TEAM TO THE SURFACE AND USE TRICORDERS TO LOCATE HIM.

I CAN HAVE A TEAM TOGETHER IN TEN MINUTES.

MM. IT'S RISKY, NUMBER ONE. I HAD HOPED FOR AN ELEGANT SOLUTION—JUST PLUCK HIM OUT OF THERE.

AND WE'RE STILL PUSHING FOR A DIPLOMATIC SOLUTION...

I DO STILL FEEL THE DOROSSHIANS CAN BE REASONED WITH IF—

ERRT ERRT

RED ALERT, WHAT—?

ENSIGN— WHAT'S GOING ON?

MISSILES, SIR. DOROSSH HAS LAUNCHED A FULL BATTERY OF MISSILES.

RIGHT IN FRONT OF US, COMMANDER. BEARING 005, MARK 330.

UNBELIEVABLE.

SHIELDS UP.

WHERE ARE THEY, ENSIGN?

THEY ARE AN ANCIENT DESIGN, CAPTAIN. OUR SHIELDS CAN DEFLECT DOZENS OF THEM WITH LITTLE TO NO LOSS.

BUT THERE ARE HUNDREDS—AND THEY'RE NOT AIMED AT US.

WHAT? THEN WHAT ARE THEY—

THEY'RE AIMED AT THE JUULETIAN SHIP UNDER US, SIR—

SOUNDS LIKE WORIKK RAN OUT OF PATIENCE.

TACTICAL— EXTEND SHIELDS OVER THE JUULETIAN SHIP.

HELM—

—COVER THEM WITH OUR SAUCER. BEARING 000, MARK 270.

MANEUVER COMPLETED.

BRIDGE TO ENGINEERING. I NEED SHIELDS AT *MAXIMUM.*

DISENGAGE ALL NON-CRITICAL PROCESSES. NONE OF THESE MISSILES CAN GET THROUGH.

YES, SIR, COMMANDER. DISENGAGING...

...YOU'VE GOT *FULL POWER* TO SHIELDS.

OH— OH NO, TH-THEY'RE *BACK*—

THE GHOSTS— THEY'RE *BACK!*

BEVERLY, HE'S SEEING GHOSTS AGAIN. GEORDI MUST HAVE TURNED OFF THE FIELD DAMPENER!

KEER... *K-KEER...*

I'M SO S-SORRY.

I SHOULD HAVE KNOWN... SHOULD HAVE SEEN IT...

ALL DECKS—

—BRACE FOR *IMPACT.*

DAMAGE REPORT.

88% DESTROYED, SIR. CLEANING UP THE REST WITH PHASERS.

SHIELDS HOLDING AT SEVENTY-FOUR PERCE— WHAT?

WHAT IS IT, ENSIGN?

SIR, AN ENERGY READING. IT'S *ZOOR* ENERGY. IT JUST POPPED UP—IT WASN'T THERE BEFORE.

IT'S HEADING RIGHT TOWARD US— WAIT—

MAXIMUM *SHIELDS*—

—IT'S HEADING FOR THE JUULETIAN SHIP—*THROUGH* US!

—BRACE FOR IMPACT.

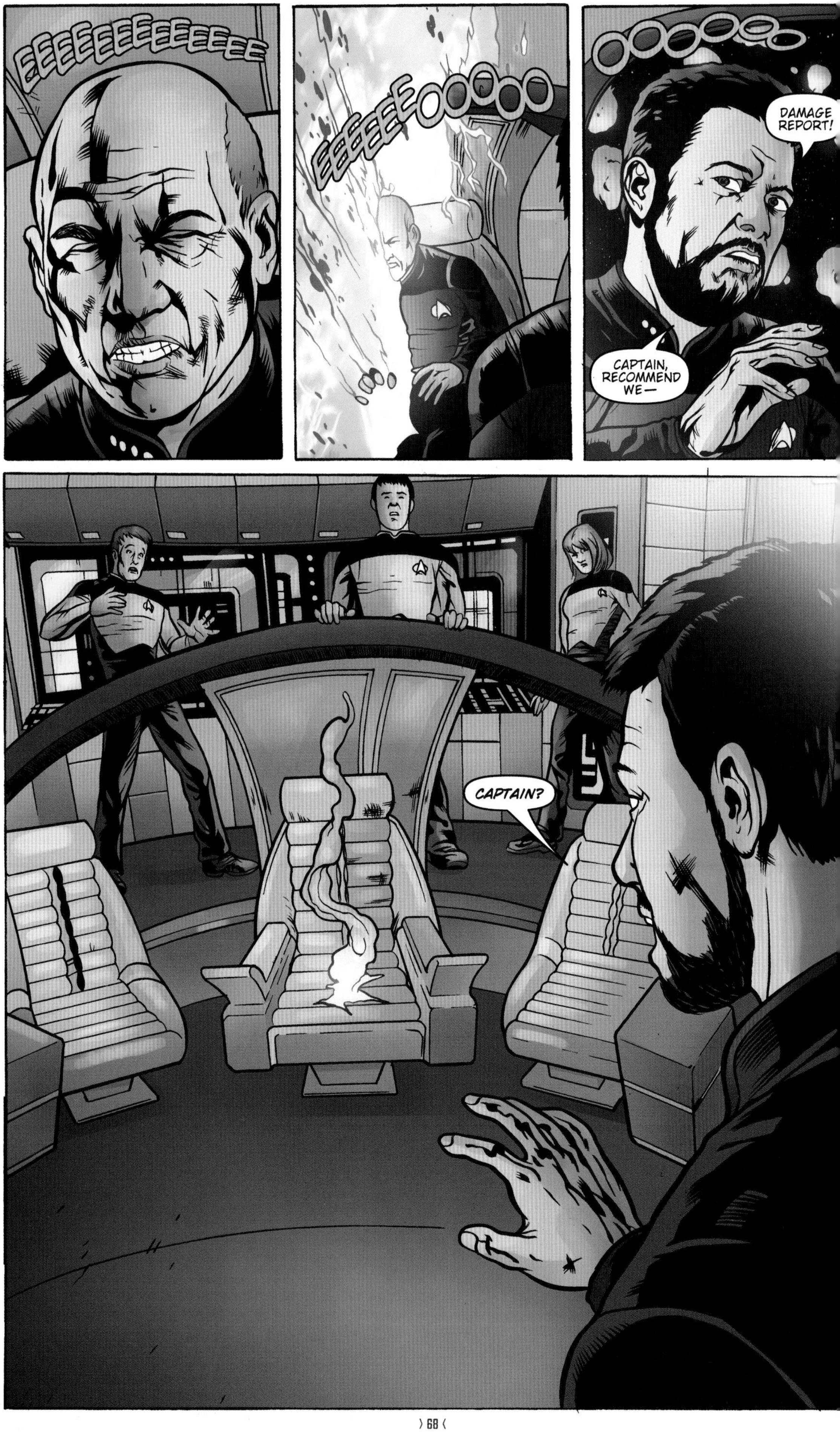
EEEEEEEEEEEEEE
EEEEEEOOOOOO
OOOOOOO
DAMAGE REPORT!
CAPTAIN, RECOMMEND WE—
CAPTAIN?

Chapter 4

FIRST OFFICER'S LOG,
STARDATE 44571.6.

CAPTAIN PICARD IS
MISSING FOLLOWING A
DEFENSIVE MANEUVER
THAT PLACED THE BRIDGE
OF THE *ENTERPRISE* IN
THE PATH OF A *ZOOR
ENERGY CLOUD*, AN
UNANTICIPATED
AFTER-EFFECT OF AN
EARLIER DISASTER.

WITH THE *MISSILE ATTACK* WHICH
PROMPTED THE DEFENSIVE MANEUVER
OVER, AND OUR CHIEF OF ENGINEERING'S
HYPOTHESIS THAT THE CAPTAIN IS LIKELY
UNHARMED, I HAVE PUT THE SHIP ON
YELLOW ALERT UNTIL WE DETERMINE
THE BEST STRATEGY FOR FINDING HIM.

LT. COMMANDER
DATA, WHAT CAN YOU
TELL ME ABOUT THE
ENERGY CLOUD'S
EFFECT ON THE
BRIDGE?

LIKE THE OTHER
SITES, COMMANDER,
IT SEEMS TO HAVE
HAD NO EFFECT ON
THE SURROUNDING
ARCHITECTURE.

I DETECT NO
RESIDUAL ENERGY,
EITHER. IT SEEMS TO
HAVE SHIFTED THE CAPTAIN
SOMEWHERE *ELSE* AND
THEN CONTINUED ON,
LEAVING THINGS AS
THEY *WERE.*

WHAT ABOUT THE CLOUD? IS IT STILL INTACT?

IS IT STILL ON ITS PATH AROUND THE PLANET?

FROM *OUR* PERSPECTIVE, *YES*, SIR. HOWEVER, THE CLOUD IS ACTUALLY *STATIONARY* RELATIVE TO THE PLANET'S CORE.

RATHER, *WE* HAVE CONTINUED ON *OUR* ORBITAL PATH AND LEFT IT BEHIND.

ALL RIGHT, HOW LONG UNTIL WE ENCOUNTER IT AGAIN?

ONE FULL DAY, SIR. THIRTY-SIX OF THEIR HOURS, THIRTY POINT TWO SIX OF OURS.

RECOMMEND WE MOVE THE *ENTERPRISE* AND THE JUULETIANS' SHIP TO A HIGHER ORBIT IN ADVANCE OF THAT TIME.

AGREED. HELM, REORIENT US AND INCREASE IMPULSE BY TEN PERCENT.

TACTICAL.

YES, SIR.

HAIL THE JUULETIAN SHIP. I WANT TO TALK WITH THEM.

LA FORGE HERE, COMMANDER. GO AHEAD.

GEORDI, I THOUGHT WE'D TUNED OUR SENSORS.

WHY COULDN'T WE DETECT THAT ENERGY CLOUD UNTIL IT WAS TOO LATE?

COMMANDER, I'M *SORRY.* WE HAD BEEN DAMPENING THE *ZOOR ENERGY* ABOARD THE SHIP SO THAT DR. CRUSHER'S PATIENT COULD TALK WITH US.

HE'S OVERWHELMED WITH VISIONS OF *GHOSTS* OTHERWISE.

RIGHT. GHOSTS THAT INCLUDE THE *CAPTAIN.*

DO *NOT* REENGAGE THAT *DAMPENER.* WE NEED INFORMATION ON WHERE THESE GHOSTS ARE.

COMMANDER, I HAVE THE JUULETIAN SHIP ON SUBSPACE.

GOOD. ON SCREEN.

COMMANDER! A CLOSE CALL WITH THAT ENERGY CLOUD. I DEARLY HOPE THAT ALL OF YOUR CREW ARE—

SKIP THE *PLEASANTRIES,* DEERON.

FIRST, ARE ALL YOUR PEOPLE UNHARMED?

THEY ARE, THANK YOU. WE ANTICIPATED THE ENERGY CLOUD AND MOVED TO THE PERIPHERY OF THE SHIP.

AND WE ARE NOW IN THE PROCESS OF MOVING WITH YOU TO A HIGHER ORBIT.

IF THERE'S ANYTHING WE CAN DO FOR YOU, COMMANDER, PLEASE—

DEERON... ...YOU HAVE DONE **ENOUGH.** I NOW CONSIDER YOUR LIES AND EVASIONS A PERSONAL **INSULT.**

B-BUT PERHAPS IF I COULD SPEAK WITH CAPTAIN PICARD...

CAPTAIN PICARD HAS BEEN **VAPORIZED,** OR **SHIFTED,** OR WHATEVER IT IS THAT CLOUD DOES, DEERON. WE WILL BE TALKING WITH YOUR RESEARCHER IN OUR SICKBAY AND DETERMINING HOW TO FIND THE CAPTAIN...

...AND HOW TO GET HIM, AND WHOEVER ELSE YOUR GUNS AND NEGLIGENCE HAVE SHIFTED, BACK **HOME.**

YOUR HELP IS NO LONGER **NEEDED,** YOUR COUNTRY IS NO LONGER A PART OF THIS **MISSION.**

ONLY THE FACT THAT YOUR RIVAL COUNTRY SHOT MISSILES AT US SAVES YOU FROM A FULLER EXPRESSION OF OUR ANGER.

ENTERPRISE OUT.

TACTICAL —HAIL **DOROSSH.**

YES, SIR.

BRIDGE TO DR. CRUSHER.

CRUSHER HERE.

WITHOUT GEORDI'S DAMPENER ENGAGED, YOUR PATIENT MUST BE SEEING GHOSTS AGAIN.

YES, SIR, HE'S VERY UPSET.

NO-NO—

ALL THE GHOSTS SEEM TO BE SPEAKING TO HIM AT **ONCE.**

PLEASE, SIR, RECOMMEND WE REENGAGE THE DAMPENER SO HE CAN CALM **DOWN.**

NEGATIVE, DOCTOR, WE **NEED** HIM TO HEAR WHAT THEY ARE SAYING.

IF THE CAPTAIN'S ONE OF THEM, HE WILL TRY AND COMMUNICATE WITH US.

IS COUNSELOR TROI THERE WITH YOU?

I'M HERE, WILL.

DEANNA, I NEED YOU TO REALLY LISTEN TO THE PATIENT— CUT THROUGH ALL THE NOISE AND FIND OUT WHAT HE'S **HEARING.**

I KNOW IT WON'T BE **EASY.** THERE'S A LOT TO SIFT THROUGH, BUT WE HAVE TO FIND THE CAPTAIN.

COMMANDER, I HAVE WORIKK FROM DOROSSH ON SUBSPACE.

ONE MOMENT.

DEANNA— THE CAPTAIN **NEEDS** US, BUT NOT AS BADLY AS WE NEED **HIM.**

DOROSSH WILL NOT LISTEN TO **REASON.** WE HAVE TO FIND **KALKASS** AND THE OTHER VICTIMS OF THIS ENERGY.

WE CAN ONLY DO THIS BY FINDING THE CAPTAIN...

"...WHO I ASSUME HAS BEEN SENT TO THE SAME PLACE AS THE OTHERS."

WHAT—?

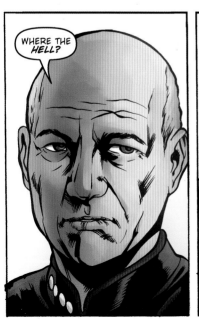

WHERE THE HELL?

PICARD TO *ENTERPRISE.* COME *IN,* ENTERPRISE.

PICARD TO—

AHOY THERE!

HELLO! OVER HERE!

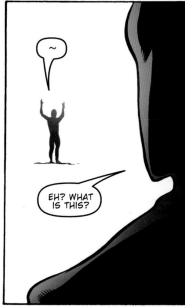
~

EH? WHAT IS THIS?

"SO, THIS IS HOW YOU OPEN NEGOTIATIONS?

WITH A **MISSILE ATTACK**, WORIKK?

FIRST YOU ARREST OUR OFFICER AND SENTENCE HIM TO DEATH WITHOUT EVIDENCE OR CAUSE.

AND NOW YOU FIRE ON US, UNPROVOKED BY ANY ACTION OF OURS.

YOU MAY BE A POWERFUL COUNTRY ON YOUR PLANET, WORIKK...

...BUT HAVE YOU ANY IDEA WHOM THIS SHIP **REPRESENTS**?

I DO, FEDERATION.

YOU REPRESENT A COLLECTION OF LIARS, FOOLS, AND HANDWRINGERS WHO SIT MANY LIFETIMES AWAY FROM US, AND AFFECT OUR FORTUNES NOT ONE BIT.

AND YOU SHOULD KNOW AS WELL AS ANYONE THAT WE WERE PROVOKED BY YOUR **INACTION**.

THE BUTCHERS FROM JUULET ARE NOT DELIVERED TO US, AND THEIR WEAPON STILL HANGS ABOVE US IN THE **SKY**.

BE IT YOU OR YOUR CAPTAIN, OR YOUR **CAPTAIN'S** CAPTAIN, I KNOW WHAT YOU REPRESENT, FEDERATION.

WORDS.

TALK, AND **LIES**.

ALL TALK AND NO **ACTION**.

WORIKK, THAT'S **ENOUGH**.

NOW IS THE TIME WHEN YOU NEED TO LISTEN TO **ME**. IGNORE THE LIEUTENANTS THAT FLANK YOU.

YOU AND I MUST SPEAK AS **LEADERS**.

CAPTAIN PICARD IS MISSING, A VICTIM OF THE ENERGY THAT WE BELIEVE ALSO CAUSED YOUR FATHER'S DISAPPEARANCE.

TWO GREAT MEN ARE *GONE*, WORIKK...

...AND SO IT IS YOU AND I WHO ARE NOW IN CHARGE.

WE MUST SPEAK QUICKLY AND UNDERSTAND WELL, FOR WE HAVE LIVES IN OUR HANDS.

THERE IS A SOLUTION HERE, WORIKK.

WE ARE CLOSE TO IT.

THE FEDERATION WILL NOT BOW TO THREATS.

NOT *EVER*.

BUT GOODWILL GESTURES ON YOUR PART WILL BE TAKEN INTO CONSIDERATION WHEN WE DETERMINE HOW THIS PLANET SHALL FARE IN THE FEDERATION'S EYES.

GOODWILL GESTURES LIKE FREEING LT. WORF.

HA!

BEFORE YOU DO YOUR UNNAMED GOOD TURN FOR US? OH, FEDERATION...

...BUT I MUST HAVE MY OFFICER BACK. AND I MUST NOT SACRIFICE ANY MORE LIVES TO DO IT.

THERE WILL BE NO *TRADE*. THERE IS ONLY A SHOW OF GOODWILL.

IT IS HOW CIVILIZED BEINGS *BEHAVE*.

...HOW NAIVE YOU MUST THINK WE ARE, HERE IN DOROSSH!

DO YOU WISH ME TO BE *ASSASSINATED* AS WELL, AFTER I DEMONSTRATE SUCH WEAKNESS?

I DO NOT, WORIKK.

I HAVE NO DESIRE TO SEE YOU LOSE FACE...

HMH. FOR A *MOMENT*, I THOUGHT YOU WERE DIFFERENT, RIKER.

A MAN OF *ACTION*, WITH A DESIRE TO *WIN*.

WE HAVE NO NEED OF YOUR *"CIVILIZATION,"* RIKER...

"...NONE OF MY PEOPLE *EVER* HAVE."

PICARD!

WHAT IS THE MEANING OF THIS?!

SUPREME ELDER KALKASS! WHAT—

THIS FEDERATION *SORCERY!* HAVE YOU BROUGHT ME TO YOUR SHIP TO—TO LIVE IN A *FALSE REALITY?*

RECREATING THE DEAD TO FOOL ME INTO REVEALING THE SECRETS OF *DOROSSH?!*

KALKASS..

GET *AWAY* FROM ME, CREATURE!

YOUR VERY PRESENCE INSULTS THE MEMORY OF ELDER *MMEMON!*

B-BUT—

I-IT'S *ME,* KALKASS!

IT'S ME, *MMEMON!* KALKASS, WHERE *ARE* WE?

WHERE HAS MY *THRONE ROOM* GONE?

NO—GET AWAY—

—THIS CANNOT *BE!*

YOU MUST BE A *SPIRIT!*

KALKASS, WH-WHAT IS THIS PLACE?

A-AND YOU—WHY DO YOU LOOK SO OLD, KALKASS?

OH NO—NO—B-BY OUR *ANCESTORS,* KALKASS...

...A-AM I *DEAD?*

YES! YES, YOU DIED SIX *QUADS* AGO, MMEMON!

KILLED BY THE TREACHEROUS *JUULETIANS!*

WE MOURNED AT YOUR *FUNERAL!*

YOU ARE *GONE,* MMEMON! YOU ARE...

NO. WE ARE ALL HERE.

WE ARE *ALL* DEAD.

PICARD...

...TELL ME THIS ISN'T SO. TELL ME YOU HAVE BROUGHT US ALL TO YOUR *SHIP* AND—

NO.

NO, KALKASS, I *CANNOT* TELL YOU IT WAS THAT.

AS FOR BEING *DEAD*...

...I DON'T KNOW.

I HAVE SEEN MUCH IN MY TRAVELS. BUT NOTHING BEYOND THE DEATH OF THE *BODY*.

AND PERHAPS...

...PERHAPS THIS IS WHAT DEATH *IS*.

NOTHINGNESS. FOREVER.

ALL ALONE.

NO. NO, WE ARE *NOT* DEAD, KALKASS.

I'M SORRY. A MOMENTARY LAPSE.

WE ARE NOT DEAD? AND WE ARE NOT ON YOUR *SHIP*?

WHERE ARE WE, PICARD? TELL ME IF YOU KNOW!

I BELIEVE WE HAVE *SHIFTED*, KALKASS, INTO ANOTHER *SPACE*.

TO TELL YOU MORE IS OUTSIDE MY AREA OF *EXPERTISE*. FOR THE DETAILS...

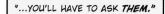

"...YOU'LL HAVE TO ASK *THEM*."

S-SO IT'S *TRUE*.

THE SPACE *EXISTS*.

WE'VE ALL READ THE THEORIES, BUT I NEVER—

MURDERERS!

WHAT—?

OH, NO...

SO, BUTCHERS, THE DEAD HAVE FOUND YOU, EH?

N-NO, AH... I AM RESEARCHER *BEEL KOSEED*.

I-I'M AS CONFUSED AS YOU—WHAT IS THIS PLACE—WHAT—

NO.

STOP YOUR *LYING*, JUULETIAN.

YOUR *ZOOR ENERGY* FROM YOUR *GUN* HAS BROUGHT US ALL HERE.

WE *KNOW*.

YOU HAVE SILENCED US, BUT NOW YOU ARE SILENT TOO, VILLAIN.

N-NOW—

AND WHO WILL COMPLAIN IN THIS PLACE IF YOU WERE TO BE *GONE*? HMM?

NO—

WHO WOULD CARE IF YOU WERE *DEAD*, MURDERER?

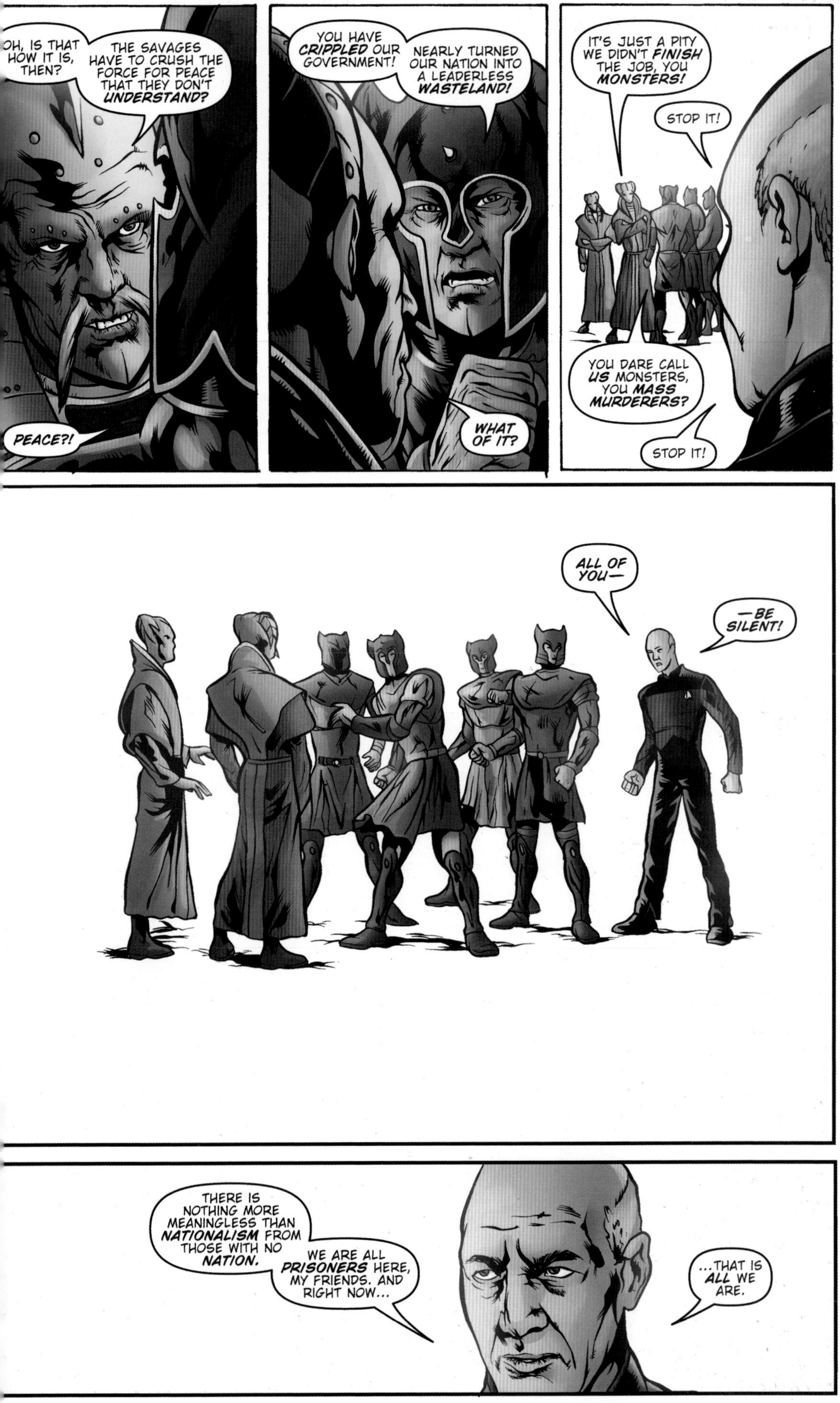
OH, IS THAT HOW IT IS, THEN?
THE SAVAGES HAVE TO CRUSH THE FORCE FOR PEACE THAT THEY DON'T UNDERSTAND?
PEACE?!
YOU HAVE CRIPPLED OUR GOVERNMENT!
NEARLY TURNED OUR NATION INTO A LEADERLESS WASTELAND!
WHAT OF IT?
IT'S JUST A PITY WE DIDN'T FINISH THE JOB, YOU MONSTERS!
STOP IT!
YOU DARE CALL US MONSTERS, YOU MASS MURDERERS?
STOP IT!
ALL OF YOU—
—BE SILENT!
THERE IS NOTHING MORE MEANINGLESS THAN NATIONALISM FROM THOSE WITH NO NATION.
WE ARE ALL PRISONERS HERE, MY FRIENDS. AND RIGHT NOW...
...THAT IS ALL WE ARE.

NO!

WE ARE HERE TOO—THIS ISN'T OUR *PRISON.*

WE DON'T KNOW *WHAT* THIS PLACE IS!

YES—PRISONERS OF THESE JUULETIAN *VILLAINS.*

ISN'T THAT *RIGHT?*

THAT'S CORRECT. NO ONE IS IN CONTROL OF THIS SPACE. NONE OF US ARE *GUARDS.*

WE SHARE THE SAME IMMEDIATE GOALS.

SO STOP FIGHTING AND LET'S FIGURE OUT OUR SITUATION.

WE HAVE ALL ARRIVED HERE SIMULTANEOUSLY, DESPITE THE FACT THAT WE DEPARTED—

OR WERE—*ATTACKED*—

YES, OR WERE *ATTACKED,* AT VERY DIFFERENT TIMES.

KALKASS, YOU REFER TO ELDER MMEMON'S "DEATH" AS BEING SIX *QUADS* AGO—I TAKE THAT TO BE APPROXIMATELY ELEVEN YEARS IN FEDERATION TIME, AND—

EXCUSE ME?

I-I DON'T KNOW WHERE *I AM.*

WHAT IS... P-PLEASE, CAN YOU *HELP* ME?

M-MY NAME IS *KEER.*

"SO, DO YOU THINK HE'S TOLD THEM ABOUT HIS *WIFE?*"

IF HE HASN'T YET, HE ALMOST CERTAINLY WILL SOON. THEY HAVE BEEN ATTENDING TO HIM NONSTOP SINCE THE ACCIDENT.

HE'S SURE TO CONFIDE IN ONE OF THEM EVENTUALLY, DESPITE OUR WARNING.

-:SIGH:-

WHAT IS IT, DEERON?

TERRIBLE TIMING. ANOTHER FEW DAYS AND WE WOULD HAVE CLEANED UP THIS MESS OURSELVES.

BUT THE *FEDERATION* HAD TO SHOW UP, AND KEJAAL IS SO INTENT ON JOINING THEM.

WITH ALL OF THE WARLORDS OUT OF THE WAY, WE DON'T *NEED* THE FEDERATION'S TECHNOLOGY...

"...BUT WITH THE FEDERATION WATCHING OVER US, WE HAVE TO LIVE BY THEIR *RULES.*

"WE'RE TOO YOUNG A COUNTRY TO DO EVERYTHING EXACTLY RIGHT. A FEW QUADS DOWN THE LINE AND OUR ETHICAL SLIPS WILL BE FORGOTTEN...

"...BUT IF UUL TELLS THEM EVERYTHING HE KNOWS, THERE'S NO SKIPPING AHEAD.

TECHNICIAN DINAAN, HAVE YOU GOT THE TRACKING CHIP'S BEARING?

YES, DEERON, AND THE FEEDBACK INDICATES IT'S STILL IN HIS *HAND.*

OKAY, THEN...

"...GOODBYE, UUL."

I'VE BEEN GONE...

...H-HOW LONG?

TWELVE *QUADS*, KEER. OVER TWENTY YEARS BY THE *FEDERATION'S* CALENDAR. I'M SORRY—THIS MUST COME AS A *SHOCK*.

—BUT MAYBE—MAYBE Y-YOU'VE ALL COME *BACK* TO *MY* TIME. O-OR WE'RE ALL COMPLETELY *DETACHED* FROM TIME.

W-WE CAN'T *KNOW*, CAN WE?

O-OUR RESEARCH IS SO INCOMPLETE O-ON THE ORE.

OH.

OH, *NO.*

UUL—M-MY *HUSBAND.* MY HUSBAND— I-IS HE...

...I-IS HE STILL *ALIVE?*

YES.

HE IS.

OHH... THANK THE *C-CORE...*

BUT, KEER...

...UUL IS THE REASON WE BELIEVE WE'RE ANCHORED IN YOUR FUTURE, MY *PRESENT.*

UUL HAS BEEN INJURED, KEER, BY THE SAME ENERGY THAT BROUGHT US HERE.

HE LIE'S IN MY SHIPS SICK BAY—

—WHERE HE IS HAUNTED BY VISIONS OF *GHOSTS.*

GHOSTS?

YES, THE GHOSTS ARE *ALL* OF *US*, KEER.

I BELIEVE HE IS **STUCK**, KEER, BETWEEN THIS WORLD AND OURS.

AND HE IS ANCHORING THEM TOGETHER.

WE NEED TO FIND HIM—OR THE PART OF HIM THAT IS IN THIS SPACE.

COMMUNICATION WITH HIM IS OUR WAY **OUT**, BACK TO THE **REAL** WORLD.

IF WE—

PICARD!

WHY DO YOU SPEND SO MUCH TIME MOLLYCODDLING THIS **ASSASSIN** FROM OUR GREAT ENEMY? WE HAVE TO RETURN TO OUR BELOVED DOROSSH—WITH **ME** GONE, WHO **KNOWS** WHAT HAS BEFALLEN IT!

KALKASS.

THIS WOMAN HAS JUST BEEN TOLD HER HUSBAND HAS LIVED HALF HIS LIFE THINKING SHE IS **DEAD**.

SHOW SOME **RESPECT**.

AND SHE IS A SCIENTIST, KALKASS. SHE'S NO MORE AN ASSASSIN THAN I AM.

HMH.

AS FOR WHAT HAS BEFALLEN DOROSSH, YOU ARE **CORRECT**.

WORIKK HAS SEIZED POWER AND ARRESTED OUR LT. WORF—FOR YOUR **MURDER**.

SO YES, WE DO NEED TO GET BACK. IF WORF DIES, I ASSURE YOU, AND I DO NOT SAY THIS LIGHTLY...

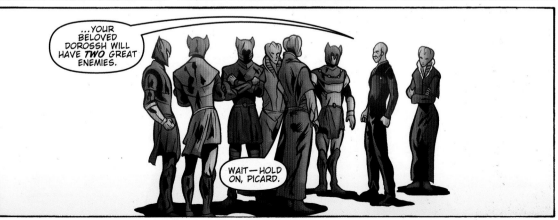

...YOUR BELOVED DOROSSH WILL HAVE **TWO** GREAT ENEMIES.

WAIT—HOLD ON, PICARD.

UUL *SURVIVED* THE EXPLOSION?

WELL, YES, BEEL, HE DID...

...ONLY IN THE SENSE THAT YOU DID *NOT*.

HE WAS MERELY *INJURED* IN THE BLAST—IT REMOVED AN ARM AND A *LEG*.

AN ARM AND A LEG THAT ARE NOW SOMEWHERE IN THIS *SPACE*.

ALL RIGHT. WE CAN FIND THEM MORE QUICKLY IF WE SPLIT INTO *GROUPS*.

STAY WITHIN SIGHT OF THE OTHER GROUPS AT ALL TIMES.

SIGNAL IF YOU FIND ANYTHING.

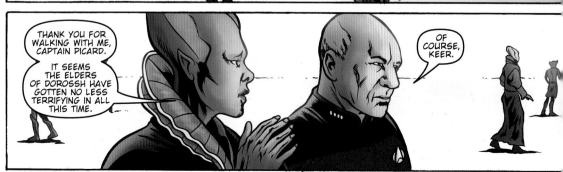

THANK YOU FOR WALKING WITH ME, CAPTAIN PICARD.

IT SEEMS THE ELDERS OF DOROSSH HAVE GOTTEN NO LESS TERRIFYING IN ALL THIS TIME.

OF COURSE, KEER.

AND THESE RESEARCHERS FROM JUULET—THEY SEEM... *FOOLISH*. HA, I'M PROBABLY AS OLD AS THEIR *MOTHERS*.

ANYWAY, I KNOW IT'S STRANGE, BUT...

...I'D RATHER SPEAK TO YOU.

I-I JUST SAW UUL *TODAY*—WELL, MY TODAY. BEFORE I CAME TO THE *LAB*.

WE'VE JUST BEEN MARRIED A LITTLE OVER A QUAD NOW—WE HAVEN'T HAD ENOUGH *TIME* TOGETHER, CAPTAIN...

AND NOW...

...BACK IN *YOUR* TIME...

...HE'LL BE SO MUCH *OLDER* THAN I AM.

I DON'T KNOW—IT'S SO STRANGE TO SKIP AHEAD LIKE THIS—TO IGNORE EVERYTHING IN BETWEEN.

OUR EARLY TIMES ARE SO FRESH IN MY MIND...

...FLIRTING ACROSS THE ROOM IN A LONG BRIEFING.

BRUSHING OUR HANDS TOGETHER AS WE PASSED...

...BUT I'M SURE HE'S FORGOTTEN ALL OF THAT. IT'S ANOTHER LIFETIME TO HIM.

KEER—

—I CAN'T SAY WHAT'S IN UUL'S MIND.

BUT FROM WHAT I'VE SEEN, HE HAS FORGOTTEN *NOTHING*.

AND ALL THE YEARS BETWEEN YOU WILL BE *GONE*—

"—WHEN HE CAN HOLD YOU AGAIN IN HIS ARMS."

HERE! OVER *HERE*!

HELLO!

MURDERER! GET US *OUT* OF HERE!

YES! USE YOUR FOUL SORCERY TO GET US *HOME!*

CAPTAIN PICARD, IT'S NO USE *REASONING* WITH THEM...

...THESE SAVAGES DON'T UNDERSTAND THAT UUL CAN'T DO ANYTHING. THEY—

ALL RIGHT, ALL RIGHT. LET'S LET KEER SEE HER HUSBAND FOR A MOMENT.

PLEASE—LET ME *THROUGH*—

PLEA—

OH... OH, UUL...

...I-IT'S *WARM*—IT'S *ALIVE.*

HE'S *ALIVE*—HE'S HERE WITH US.

ALL RIGHT, PICARD, NOW HOW DO WE *TALK* TO YOUR PEOPLE THROUGH HIM?

I SAID ONE *MOMENT*, BEEL.

UUL—CAN YOU *FEEL* THIS? WHEN I SQUEEZE YOUR *HAND*—

CAN YOU SQUEEZE IT B—

H-HE *DID.*

HE'S *THERE.* HE CAN *FEEL* ME HERE.

WE CAN *TALK.*

I-IT'S *KEER*.

SHE'S HERE.

SHE'S *ALIVE*.

TH-THE *TALKING*... ALL THE TALKING IS STILL SO CONFUSING, BUT—

B-BUT NOW SHE'S HOLDING MY *HAND*...

YES, I FEEL YOU CALMING *DOWN*, UUL...

Y-YES. F-FOR THE F-FIRST TIME, I FEEL LIKE IT'S ALL GOING TO BE ALL R—

NNH—

UUL?!

DEANNA—HIS VITALS JUST *DROPPED*.

XIAN—PREPARE A HYPOSPRAY OF—

NO—JUST A MOMENT—I FEEL HIM COMING BACK TO *NORMAL*.

UUL? ARE YOU ALL RIGHT? WHAT *HAPPENED*?

I-I DON'T KNOW. I... UH... I JUST FELT S-S-SOMETHING *HIT* ME FOR A MOMENT...

...I-I DON'T KNOW WHAT IT COULD *BE*..

BIP ZOOR

?

WHAT THE—?

ZOOR ENERGY

LA FORGE TO BRIDGE.

FOR THE LAST TIME, WORIKK, RETURN LT. WORF, OR—

HA! OR **WHAT**, RIKER?

YOU HAVE DEMONSTRATED ON NUMEROUS OCCASIONS WE HAVE NOTHING TO FEAR FROM THE GUTLESS FEDERATION.

REPEAT— LA FORGE TO **BRIDGE**.

TACTICAL— CUT AUDIO TRANSMISSION.

WHAT IS IT, GEORDI?

COMMANDER —WE'VE GOT ANOTHER ZOOR ENERGY READING.

WHAT'S THE **SOURCE**?

IT'S THE JUULETIANS' SHIP, SIR. IT'S A VERY WEAK BEAM—THEY PROBABLY FIGURE IT'S BELOW OUR SENSORS' **THRESHOLD**.

BUT IT'S AIMED AT US, SPECIFICALLY, AT **SICK BAY**.

THAT IS **IT**.

I WANT A SECURITY DETAIL TO THE **BRIG**.

YES, SIR.

BRIDGE TO TRANSPORTER ROOM.

O'BRIEN HERE, COMMANDER.

O'BRIEN— HOW MANY CREW MEMBERS ARE ABOARD THE JUULETIANS' SHIP?

I'M READING... **THREE**, SIR.

LOCK ONTO THEM AND BEAM THEM DIRECTLY TO A **HOLDING CELL**.

TACTICAL.

SIR.

TARGET THE **SHIP**.

Y-YES, SIR.

B-BUT WHAT SHALL I HAVE THE SECURITY TEAM TELL THE **JUULETIANS**?

LET 'EM **WONDER**.

FIRE.

CLAP CLAP CLAP

BRAVO, RIKER.

WHAT—?

I GUESS I WAS RIGHT ABOUT YOU ALL *ALONG.*

A MAN OF *ACTION.*

NOW, YOU'VE MET ONE OF OUR TWO CRITERIA FOR FREEING YOUR ASSASSIN *WORF.*

IMPOSSIBLE, YOU SAID. AND YET IT IS DONE.

TACTICAL—END TRANSMISSION.

PERHAPS IN THE END, COMMANDER—

—YOU AND I ARE NOT SO DIFFERENT—

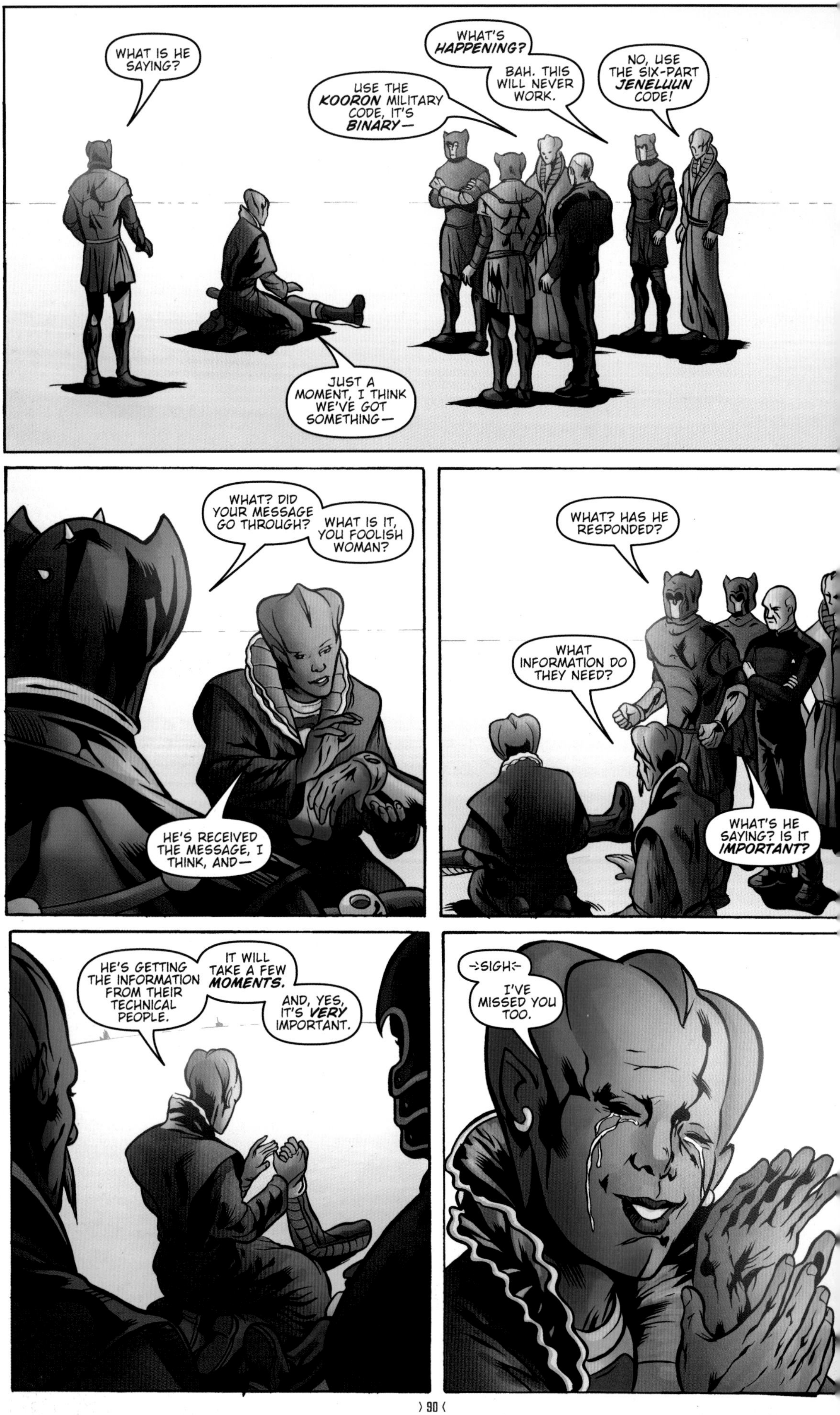
WHAT IS HE SAYING?
USE THE KOORON MILITARY CODE, IT'S BINARY—
WHAT'S HAPPENING?
BAH. THIS WILL NEVER WORK.
NO, USE THE SIX-PART JENELUUN CODE!
JUST A MOMENT, I THINK WE'VE GOT SOMETHING—
WHAT? DID YOUR MESSAGE GO THROUGH?
WHAT IS IT, YOU FOOLISH WOMAN?
HE'S RECEIVED THE MESSAGE, I THINK, AND—
WHAT? HAS HE RESPONDED?
WHAT INFORMATION DO THEY NEED?
WHAT'S HE SAYING? IS IT IMPORTANT?
HE'S GETTING THE INFORMATION FROM THEIR TECHNICAL PEOPLE.
IT WILL TAKE A FEW MOMENTS.
AND, YES, IT'S VERY IMPORTANT.
-SIGH-
I'VE MISSED YOU TOO.

Chapter 5

FIRST OFFICER'S LOG, STARDATE 44751.7.

THE SITUATION ABOVE ALLIOS IV HAS REACHED CRISIS LEVELS.

THE CURRENT WARLORD OF THE PRIMITIVE NATION OF DOROSSH, WORIKK, HAS SET A TIME FOR THE CAPTURED AND FALSELY ACCUSED LT. WORF'S EXECUTION: SUNDOWN *TONIGHT.*

ALL OF OUR DIPLOMACY HAS AMOUNTED TO NOTHING WHILE DEALING WITH A LEADER SO SHORTSIGHTED AS TO CARE NOTHING FOR CONSEQUENCES.

OUR TRACKING TECHNOLOGY HAS BEEN USELESS WHEN CONFRONTED WITH A CITY SO DENSE AND SO CHAOTIC THAT WORF COULD BE LITERALLY ANYWHERE.

ELEGANT SOLUTIONS HAVE FAILED US.

I FEEL THAT THE ANSWER LIES IN TACTICS THAT RELY LESS ON MATHEMATICS AND PROBABILITY AND MORE ON DIRECT CONTACT.

I'VE SENT A CREWMEMBER DOWN TO AGGRESSIVELY INVESTIGATE THE LIKELIEST POSSIBILITIES.

TO BRING THE *HUMAN* TOUCH.

I AM SURE CAPTAIN PICARD WOULD NOT HAVE MADE THE SAME DECISION, BUT HE IS MISSING, FOLLOWING THE *ENTERPRISE'S* ENCOUNTER WITH A CLOUD OF ENERGY, THE RESIDUE OF AN EARLIER ACCIDENT.

THE ENERGY HAS DEPOSITED HIM IN A POCKET DIMENSION, ALONG WITH A NUMBER OF OTHER VICTIMS.

HOW WE KNOW THIS IS DUE TO *UUL EVERUUD*, WHO WAS WOUNDED BY AN EARLIER ENERGY CLOUD AND NOW IS SPLIT BETWEEN THAT WORLD AND OURS.

USING UUL'S BODY AS A CONDUIT, PICARD AND THE OTHERS ARE ABLE TO COMMUNICATE WITH OUR SICK BAY. CHIEF ENGINEER GEORDI LA FORGE HAS THE TASK OF REVISING A PHYSICAL LINK TO THE SPACE.

THOSE RESPONSIBLE FOR THE ENERGY MISHAPS HAVE BEEN DETAINED IN OUR BRIG, AFTER ATTEMPTING TO SILENCE UUL WITH ANOTHER ENERGY BURST.

THIS IS ALL A *MISTAKE!*

I DEMAND TO SEE COMMANDER *RIKER.*

I'VE BEEN INSTRUCTED NOT TO SPEAK WITH YOU, SIR.

OKAY, UUL, THE BEAM HAS STOPPED, YOU'RE SAFE. JUST FOCUS ON MY *VOICE*.

NOW, WHAT'S THE NEXT MESSAGE?

I-IT'S— IT'S T-THREE SEVEN SIX NINE TWELVE FOUR ONE. TH-THEN THE NEXT S-SEQUENCE—

—FOUR TEN EIGHT FIVE ELEVEN SIX NINE.

GEORDI, ARE YOU GETTING THIS?

I'M GETTING IT DOWN, BUT IT'S NOT MAKING *SENSE*.

THESE NUMBER SEQUENCES...

...THEY HAVE THE RIGHT *SYNTAX* FOR A COORDINATE OR A BEARING OR SOMETHING, BUT...

...I DON'T KNOW—I MEAN, *ELEVEN*?

THAT JUST DOESN'T FIT—A DOUBLE DIGIT NUMBER IN THE SEQUENCE. I—

WAIT, HOLD ON, EVERYONE—

—LOOK AT HIS LEG!

I SEE IT, TOO—THE GLOW, IT'S *MOVING*, SPREADING...

UUL, ARE YOU ALL *RIGHT*?

WH-WHAT? I-I'M SORRY...

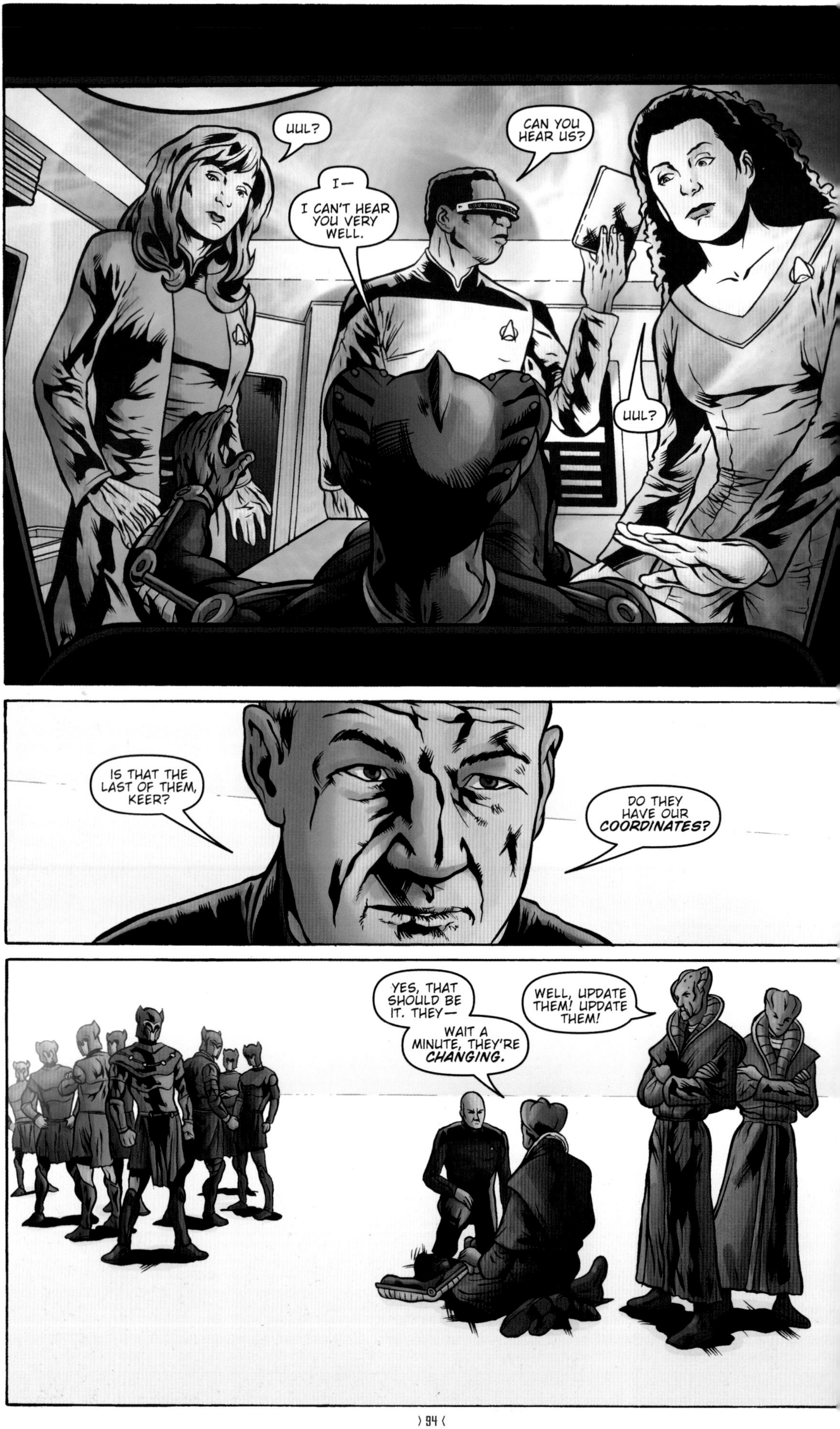
UUL?
CAN YOU HEAR US?
I— I CAN'T HEAR YOU VERY WELL.
UUL?
IS THAT THE LAST OF THEM, KEER?
DO THEY HAVE OUR COORDINATES?
YES, THAT SHOULD BE IT. THEY—
WAIT A MINUTE, THEY'RE CHANGING.
WELL, UPDATE THEM! UPDATE THEM!

LOOK, I DON'T EVEN KNOW WHAT THESE NUMBERS ARE SUPPOSED TO *MEAN*.

THIS GADGET... THE IDEA OF THIS *SPACE* MAY BE SIMPLE TO *YOU*...

...BUT IT'S ALL STUFF THAT'S NEVER BEEN *DREAMED* OF IN MY TIME.

WE'VE ONLY JUST *DISCOVERED* ZOOR ENERGY.

YOU'VE HAD IT ALMOST YOUR WHOLE *LIFE*.

JUST *UPDATE* THEM, WILL YOU?

HMH. YOU KNOW...

UUL AND I HAVE... WELL, I GUESS WE *HAD* SUCH DREAMS ABOUT WHAT TO DO WITH THIS ENERGY.

OTHER ORES IN THE CRUST OF THE PLANET WERE VALUABLE FOR TRADE, BUT *THIS*...

...THIS COULD CHANGE *EVERYTHING*. TRANSPORTATION, COMMUNICATION, WASTE-MANAGEMENT.

EVERYTHING.

WE JUST HAD TO EXAMINE ITS EFFECTS ON—

YEAH, SURE. TYPICAL *FEMALE.*

OBSESSING OVER TECHNICAL DETAILS WHEN THE ANSWERS ARE RIGHT IN FRONT OF YOU.

WHAT?

LOOK AT THEM, KEER.

YOU THINK YOUR NOTIONS OF HOW TO USE THE ENERGY WILL DO US ANY GOOD WITH *THEM* MASSING AT OUR GATES?

DEERON HAS A VISION OF THE FUTURE, TOO. A FAR MORE REALISTIC ONE.

AND IT SOLVES THE PROBLEM WE HAVE *NOW*. THE *DOROSSHIANS*.

WAIT. THEN ALL OF US COMING TO THIS PLACE—YOU TWO, AND CAPTAIN PICARD AND I...

...WE'RE ALL HERE DUE TO ACCIDENTS, BUT—

—BUT THE DOROSSHIANS?

HOW DID *THEY* GET HERE?

COME ON, KEER. CAN'T YOU *GUESS*?

Y-YOU *MURDERED* THEM?

MURDERED? WHAT, DON'T YOU SEE THEM THERE?

BUT THEIR FAMILIES, THEIR LIVES—EVERYONE THINKS THEY ARE DEAD, THEY ARE FORGOTTEN.

YOU DON'T CALL *THAT* MURDERED?

THIS ORE—THIS ENERGY—IT COULD HAVE PUT US ON PAR WITH THE CORE SYSTEMS... BUT ALL YOU COULD THINK TO DO WITH IT IS KILL OUR *NEIGHBORS*.

HOW *COULD* YOU?

HOW COULD *I*, KEER?

DON'T BE SO *MODEST*...

IT'S ONLY THANKS TO YOU THAT WE COULD DO ANY OF THIS AT ALL.

YOUR EXTREME TECHNICAL EXPERTISE...

"...YOU MADE THIS POSSIBLE."

KKRK KNEW YOU WOULD HAIL US AGAIN, COMMANDER RIKER.

SO FRUSTRATING, ISN'T IT, THAT YOU STILL DON'T KNOW WHERE WE ARE?

KK SUNDOWN DRAWS *CLOSER*, RIKER.

YOUR OFFICER SITS SILENTLY, NO DOUBT CONTEMPLATING HIS DEATH. A PITY YOU HAVEN'T THE EXPEDIENCY TO PREVENT IT.

SKRK YOU HAVE THE JUULETIAN FUNCTIONARY DEERON IN YOUR BRIG, COMMANDER. I KNOW THIS.

YOUR SURRENDERING DEERON...

...WOULD LIFT THE SWORD AWAY FROM YOUR LT. WORF'S NECK.

AT LEAST BUY YOU MORE *TIME*.

YOU AND DEERON DO NOT SHARE A GREAT FRIENDSHIP, RIKER. YOU DETONATED HIS GUNSHIP AT OUR REQUEST.

WOULD IT TROUBLE YOU TO TURN HIM OVER TO US?

I DO *NOTHING* AT YOUR REQUEST, WORIKK.

I SIMPLY HAVE THE FEDERATION'S REASONS, AND MY OWN.

DEERON WILL NOT BE SURRENDERED, NOT EVEN AT THE COST OF OUR CREWMAN'S LIFE.

YOU IN YOUR SHINY SKY-VESSELS MAY THINK US SAVAGES, RIKER...

...BUT OUR TIME IS STILL VALUABLE TO US KRK—

VKGKKSKK MKKSUKKVK GHKK MGKKHK

VKKGHK GKK KSK KGON'T KNOW WHY YOU BOTHER HAILING US.

WORIKK OUT.

DATA TO ENTERPRISE.

GO AHEAD, COMMANDER.

INTERFERENCE BEACON HAS BEEN ACTIVATED AT SITE C. IT WILL EMIT ITS SIGNAL AT FORTY-SECOND INTERVALS.

ACKNOWLEDGED.

YOU ARE CLEARED TO POWER DOWN THE BEACON, COMMANDER.

THE BRIDGE REPORTS THE SIGNAL AT 0142 HOURS PRODUCED SIGNIFICANT DISRUPTION.

YOU ARE NOW WITHIN A THREE-KILOMETER RADIUS OF WORIKK'S BROADCAST LOCATION.

THIRD TIME'S A CHARM, EH?

CHIEF O'BRIEN, NUMERICAL MILESTONES HAVE NO EFFECT ON THE STATISTICAL PROBABILITY OF—

—ERR, RIGHT, COMMANDER. ANYWAY, WE'RE SHOWING THAT THE SUN WILL SET ON ALLIOS IV AT 0226 HOURS.

YOU HAVE FORTY-FOUR MINUTES UNTIL WORF IS SCHEDULED TO BE EXECUTED.

WE WILL BE WORKING AS QUICKLY AS POSSIBLE TO SIFT THROUGH THE LIFE-FORMS IN THE RADIUS WITH OUR SENSORS, BUT DATA...

...WE'RE COUNTING ON YOU.

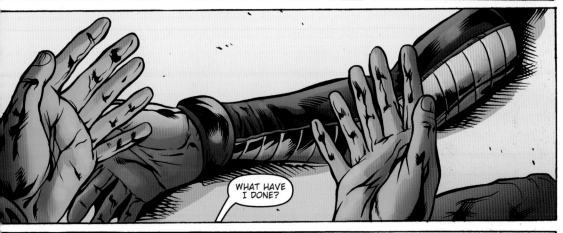

WHAT HAVE I DONE?

CAPTAIN PICARD—ALL WE WANTED WAS TO DISCOVER THIS ENERGY AND HARNESS IT—

SOMETHING TO SET ALLIOS IV—AND JUULET—APART. SOMETHING TO MAKE US MORE THAN JUST A PLANET OF *MINERS.*

SOMETHING TO MAKE US MOVE FORWARD—*CIVILIZE* US.

BUT YOU FEEL ALL YOU'VE ACCOMPLISHED IS TO GIVE EVERYONE MORE WAYS TO HURT EACH OTHER.

I SUPPOSE IT'S FITTING TO BE SENT HERE AS PUNISHMENT...

...FOR MY ROLE IN CREATING THIS WEAPON.

...I KNOW A THING OR TWO ABOUT GETTING OUT OF ONE'S DEPTH.

KEER...

OFTEN THE BEST OF INTENTIONS SETS INTO MOTION THE WORST DISASTERS.

I HAVE PUT ONE OF MY CREW IN HARM'S WAY BY INVESTIGATING THESE EVENTS.

HE MAY SOON DIE AT THE HANDS OF THE DOROSSHIANS.

HE HOLDS STRONG SPIRITUAL BELIEFS, KEER.

TO DIE AS A CAPTIVE IS DISGRACEFUL TO HIM, AND HE BELIEVES HIS SPIRIT WILL BE SENT TO HIS PEOPLE'S LAND OF THE DISHONORED DEAD.

"IT IS NOT UNLIKE THIS PLACE, IN A WAY.

"WHEN I FIRST ARRIVED HERE, I TOO BELIEVED IT WAS PUNISHMENT FOR RISKING WORF—AND COUNTLESS OTHERS—OVER MY CAREER.

"BUT LIKE MANY THINGS IN LIFE, WHAT SEEMS LIKE A PUNISHMENT IS SIMPLY A *TEST*.

"WE ARE STILL ALIVE.

"WE MAY STILL CHANGE OUR FORTUNE.

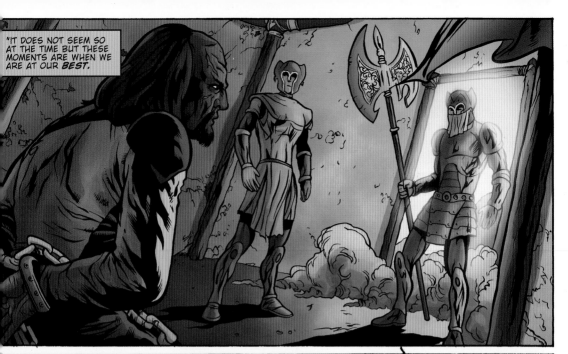

"IT DOES NOT SEEM SO AT THE TIME BUT THESE MOMENTS ARE WHEN WE ARE AT OUR *BEST*.

"WHEN WE SEE THE WORLD IN EXTRA SHARP FOCUS...

"...AND INDECISION FALLS AWAY FOR A MOMENT ...

"...SHOWING US THE STRAIGHT PATH TO THE ANSWER."

I DON'T GET IT.

WE'VE GOT THE TRANSPORTERS POWERED UP.

THE NAV COMPUTERS ARE TRACKING THE COORDINATES I'VE ENTERED.

BUT HIS NUMBERS—THEY DON'T MAKE SENSE.

THE DOUBLE DIGITS...

GEORDI—WE'RE LOSING UUL—HE'S FADING AWAY.

YOU HAVE TO DO SOMETHING. WE HAVE TO BEAM THEM OUT OF THERE.

EVERYONE! IN HERE!

SUBDUE THE FEDERATION ASSASSIN!!

GEORDI—UUL'S THE ONLY THING ANCHORING THOSE PEOPLE TO THE PRESENT.

IF HE'S CONSUMED BEFORE THEY'RE OUT—

I KNOW!

I'M THINKING!

THE ENERGY IS GOING TO GET TO HIS VITAL ORGANS, SOON.

WHEN IT WAS JUST AT HIS EXTREMITIES WE COULD DAMPEN, BUT IF IT GETS—

I KNOW, IT'S—WAIT—

HIS EXTREMITIES!

OF COURSE

HE WAS SHACKLED AT THE WRISTS—

—DAMN IT, HOW DID HE SLIP FREE?!

THEIR *HANDS!*

THEY HAVE SIX *FINGERS!*

BUT WHAT—

TWELVE TOTAL, BEVERLY— THEY'RE USING A BASE-12 NUMBER SYSTEM!

COMPUTER!

ADJUST ALL CALCULATIONS TO BASE *TWELVE* AND BEGIN LOCKING ONTO ANYONE AT THOSE *COORDINATES.*

WE'RE GETTING THEM OUT OF THERE *NOW!*

EXECUTIONER— —YOU HAVE *FAILED* ME.

I WILL DO THE JOB MYSELF.

GET OUT OF MY *SIGHT.*

DATA TO *ENTERPRISE*— —THE SEARCH HAS NARROWED.

I'M SURE THAT'S VERY INSPIRING, CAPTAIN PICARD.

IT'S CLEARLY PART OF YOUR JOB TO SPUR PEOPLE ON TO GREAT THINGS, BUT—

GREAT GODS *BELOW!*

WHAT IS *THAT?*

AH.

THE *ENTERPRISE.*

THEY'VE FOUND THIS SPACE.

BUT THEY MUST NOT BE ABLE TO LOCK ON TO US—THEY'RE JUST TAKING GUESSES WITH THE TRANSPORTERS.

BAH! IT'S *GONE!*

NO! THERE IT IS AGAIN!

KEER, YOU NEED TO GET A MESSAGE TO THEM THROUGH UUL.

BEEL CAN TELL THEM HOW TO REFINE THEIR *COORDINATES.*

QUICKLY!

ALL RIGHT.

OH, NO, WHAT— —CAPTAIN PICARD!

WHAT IS IT?

IT'S UUL...

...THERE'S *MORE* OF HIM.

I THINK THE ENERGY'S EATING AWAY AT HIM...

...HE'S SLOWLY BEING SHIFTED HERE *COMPLETELY.*

THEN WE HAVE NO TIME TO *WASTE!*

BEEL!

UUL...

BEEL, WE NEED YOU TO UPDATE THE COORDINATES— HELP THEM REFINE THEIR GUESSES.

BUT I DON'T—

UUL... YOU'RE BEING DRAWN HERE TOO...

ANYTHING, ANYTHING YOU CAN DO TO GET THE TRANSPORTER SIGNAL TO REMAIN STATIONARY AND *ACCESSIBLE.*

BY THIS ENERGY WE DISCOVERED TOGETHER.

ALL RIGHT, CAPTAIN PICARD.

I'LL *TRY.*

OH MY HUSBAND...

...YOU'RE BEING PUNISHED, TOO.

KEER— TELL THEM THIS SEQUENCE—

KEER...

"... DO YOU *HEAR* ME?!"

UUL?

UUL, IT'S ME, *DEANNA.*

I-I CAN'T—I-IS SOMEONE *TALKING?*

WH-WHO'S THERE?

P-PUNISHED? WHAT DO YOU *MEAN?*

N-NOW YOU'RE T-TELLING ME NUMBERS—

OH, IT'S *YOU,* KEER. OF COURSE, OF COURSE.

FOUR... ELEVEN... NINE... SIX... THREE... SEVEN... TEN.

GOT THAT, O'BRIEN?

GOT IT. ADJUSTING NOW...

UUL? UUL, I BELIEVE WE'VE GOTTEN ALL OF THE INFORMATION WE NEED.

NOW I HAVE TO TELL YOU SOMETHING.

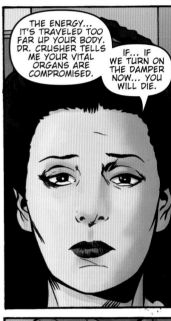

THE ENERGY... IT'S TRAVELED TOO FAR UP YOUR BODY. DR. CRUSHER TELLS ME YOUR VITAL ORGANS ARE COMPROMISED.

IF... IF WE TURN ON THE DAMPER NOW... YOU WILL DIE.

I KNOW YOU'RE CONFUSED. I KNOW YOU'RE SCARED. YOU'VE BEEN SO BRAVE IN THE FACE OF DANGER...

...SO BRAVE IN THE FACE OF YOUR COUNTRYMEN'S *THREATS.*

I-I CAN'T—

YOU DESERVE A REST. YOU DON'T HAVE TO BE BRAVE ANYMORE.

I'M HONORED TO HAVE MET YOU.

GOODBYE, UUL.

I...

WE DON'T KNOW HOW LONG THIS CAN LAST!

FORM GROUPS OF TWO—

ELDER KALKASS, WITH **ME**—

QUICKLY, ALL OF YOU!

KEER, QUICKLY!

KEER, THIS SPACE IS SHIFTING CONSTANTLY—WE HAVE TO **HURRY!**

THIS IS OUR ONLY CHANCE—

KEER?

KEER, PLEASE, YOU HAVE TO COME WITH US.

UUL IS THE ONLY THING STABILIZING US IN **TIME**.

WE ONLY HAVE A FEW MINUTES.

I WANT TO SAY THANK YOU, CAPTAIN.

YOU HAVE UNITED US IN THIS SPACE. WE WOULD BE LOST WITHOUT YOU.

YOU **SAVED** US.

BUT I CAN'T GO. I DON'T **DESERVE** TO GO.

YOU ARE A FINE LEADER. YOU WILL SURELY SAVE THOUSANDS IN YOUR JOURNEYS.

BUT PLEASE, CAPTAIN, FOR ME...

...JUST DO IT FOR THOSE WHO **WANT** SAVING.

O'BRIEN—IT'S 0224 HOURS—WHAT THE HELL IS THE HOLDUP?

THE VICTIMS ARE COMING THROUGH, COMMANDER, BUT IT'S SLOW GOING.

THE UNPREDICTABLE NATURE OF THIS SPACE THEY'RE COMING FROM—EACH DOPPLER COMPENSATION TAKES SEVERAL MINUTES AND USES AN INCREDIBLE AMOUNT OF—

DATA TO ENTERPRISE—

I HAVE DETERMINED LT. WORF'S PRECISE LOCATION. HE IS SEVEN METERS DUE SOUTH OF MY POSITION.

"ALL RIGHT, GET HIM, O'BRIEN. QUICKLY."

"SIR, WE CAN'T—"

"—GEORDI SAYS THE ENERGY EXPENDITURE FOR THIS OPERATION IS PUSHING THE CORE TO ITS LIMIT."

DAMN IT, O'BRIEN—THE SUN IS SETTING ON ALLIOS IV—WORF IS GOING TO DIE IF WE DON'T DO SOMETHING NOW!

WHO IS IN THE BUFFER?

IT'S CAPTAIN PICARD, SIR, AND A DOROSSHIAN BIOSIGN, BUT—

WHO IS IT?

I CAN'T TELL, SIR, IT'S IMPOSSIBLE—

DOESN'T MATTER. WORF'S POSITION. SEND THEM, O'BRIEN—

NOW.

NOW IS WHEN WE GIVE A **RECKONING**, FRIENDS...

A RECKONING TO THOSE WHO WOULD INTERFERE.

TO THOSE WHO WOULD **MURDER** TO SHAPE US INTO THE TYPE OF NATION THEY **PREFER.**

AND TO THOSE WHO WOULD JOIN IN A FIGHT THAT IS NOT **THEIRS.**

SOME OF YOU HAVE BEEN MOVED BY THE FEDERATION'S RETTY TALK ABOUT THIS ASSASSIN'S "NOBLE WARRIOR BELIEFS."

AND BY THEIR INSISTENCE THAT MY FATHER, **KALKASS,** IS NOT DEAD BY HIS HAND.

I TELL YOU, IT IS A **LIE** AND IT IS **NONSENSE.** THIS FOOL IS NO WARRIOR, HE IS A MERE TECHNICIAN AND HE WILL BE DEAD IN A MOMENT.

AND MY FATHER? DO THEY TAKE US FOR **RUBES?**

WE ARE INTELLIGENT BEINGS.

WE DON'T BELIEVE IN **GHOSTS.**

FAREWELL, ASSASSIN.

"BEING FACE-TO-FACE WITH HER SUPPOSEDLY DEAD FATHER MUST HAVE BEEN A BIT OF A *SHOCK*."

"INDEED.

"AND ONCE EVERYONE REALIZED KALKASS WAS REALLY FLESH AND BLOOD—"

A GOOD NUMBER OF THE THINGS KEEPING WORIKK IN POWER STARTED TO *CRUMBLE*.

AH, DOCTOR.

HOW IS WORF?

DEHYDRATED, EXHAUSTED, SOME BROKEN RIBS.

A FEW DAYS REST SHOULD HELP GREATLY, BUT HE'LL BE FINE.

YES.

HE'S A *FIGHTER*.

NOW, CAPTAIN...

...ARE *YOU* ALL RIGHT? YOU SEEM—

FINE, THANK YOU, NUMBER ONE.

JUST THINKING ABOUT THE ONE PERSON WE LEFT BEHIND.

SHE... WOULDN'T COME, AND NOW...

...SHE'S THERE ALL ALONE. FOREVER.

ALONE? WELL, CAPTAIN...

"...I'M NOT SO SURE ABOUT THAT."

WHUH?

WHERE—?

OH, NO— SH-SHE SAID GOODBYE—AND HERE I AM.

A-AND...

UUL?

WHAT—?

OH!

OH, KEER! KEER! OH, FINALLY...

CAPTAIN'S LOG, SUPPLEMENTAL:

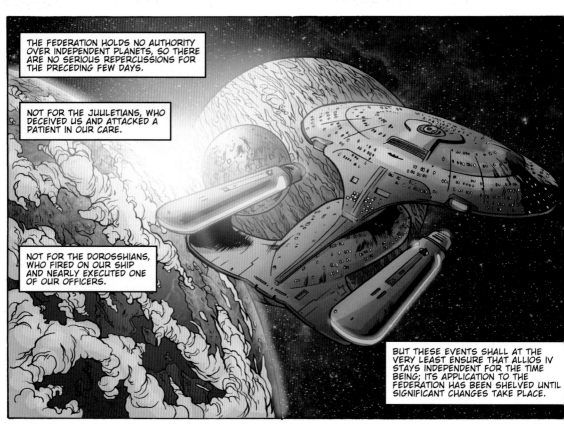

THE FEDERATION HOLDS NO AUTHORITY OVER INDEPENDENT PLANETS, SO THERE ARE NO SERIOUS REPERCUSSIONS FOR THE PRECEDING FEW DAYS.

NOT FOR THE JUULETIANS, WHO DECEIVED US AND ATTACKED A PATIENT IN OUR CARE.

NOT FOR THE DOROSSHIANS, WHO FIRED ON OUR SHIP AND NEARLY EXECUTED ONE OF OUR OFFICERS.

BUT THESE EVENTS SHALL AT THE VERY LEAST ENSURE THAT ALLIOS IV STAYS INDEPENDENT FOR THE TIME BEING; ITS APPLICATION TO THE FEDERATION HAS BEEN SHELVED UNTIL SIGNIFICANT CHANGES TAKE PLACE.

IT MAY NOT BE TOO MUCH TO HOPE FOR. THE DOROSSHIAN ELDERS HAVE SEEN THINGS FROM A NEW PERSPECTIVE, AND JUULET'S SPEAKER DAAR KEJAAL, AFTER LEARNING OF DEERON'S EXTENSIVE ASSASSINATION CAMPAIGN, HAS PLEDGED REFORM.

AND SO LIFE ABOARD THE *ENTERPRISE* CONTINUES MUCH AS IT HAS.

ENSIGN. SET A COURSE FOR QO'NOS, IN THE KLINGON SYSTEM.

THE ONLY DIFFERENCE BEING THE PEOPLE WE HAVE MET, THE INFORMATION WE HAVE LEARNED...

COURSE IS SET, CAPTAIN.

WARP FOUR.

...AND THE THINGS THAT *HAUNT* US.

ENGAGE

END

STAR TREK
THE NEXT GENERATION®
GHOSTS

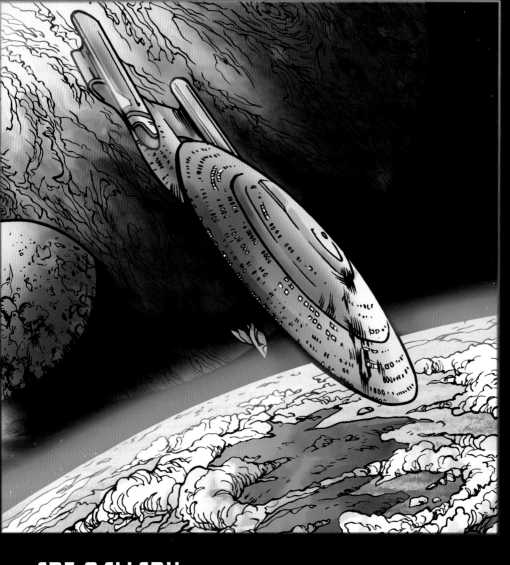

ART GALLERY
featuring Joe Corroney

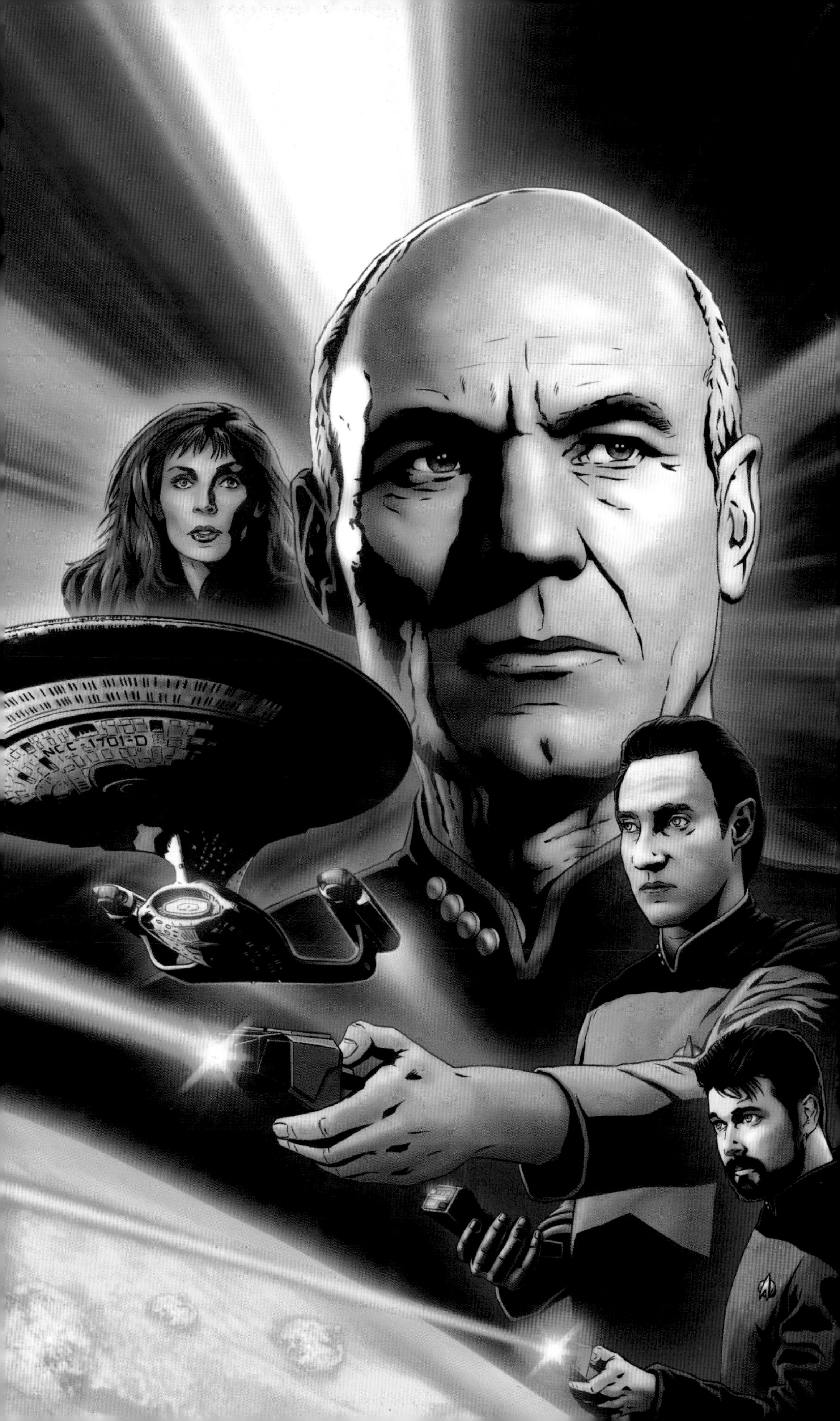
NCC-1701-D

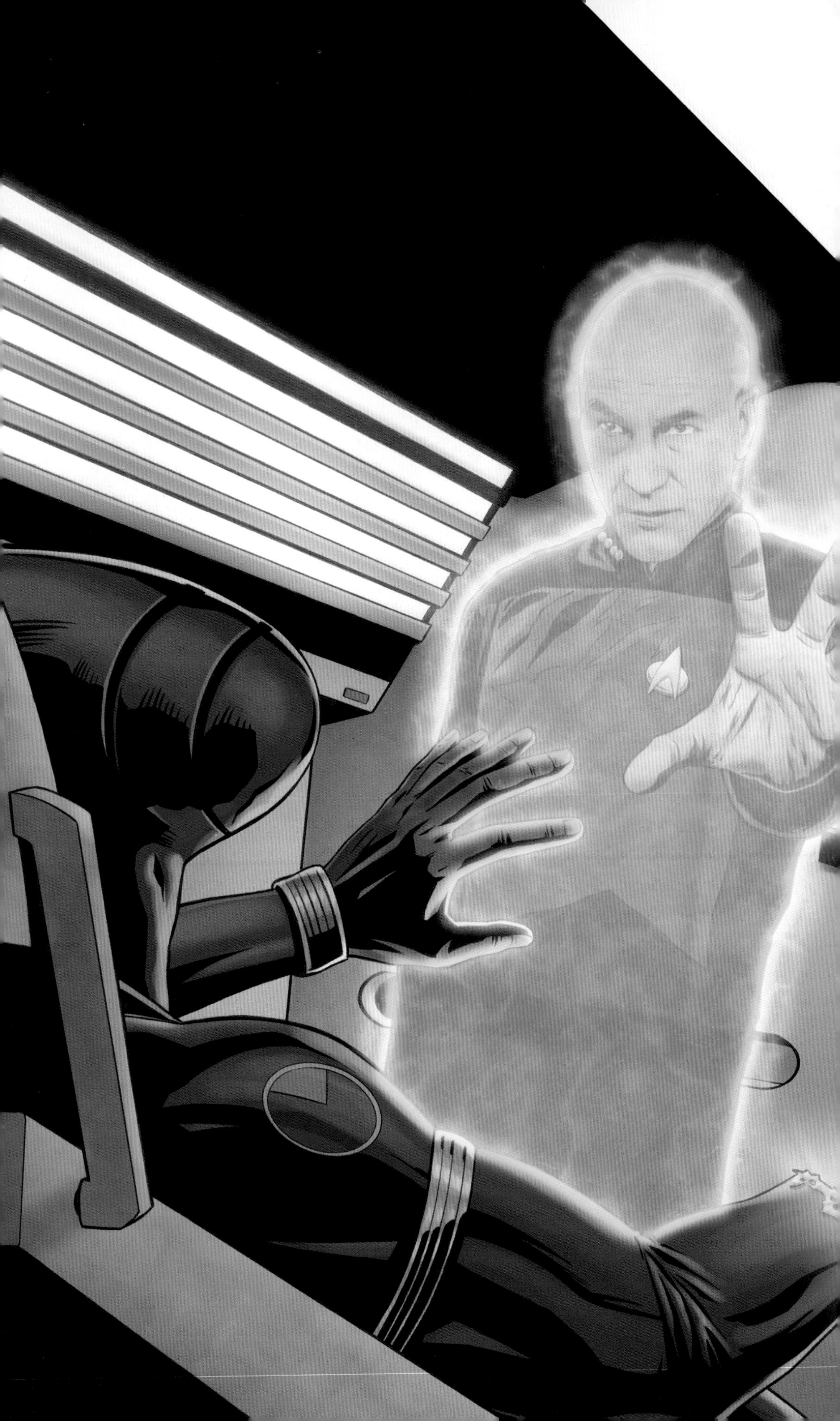

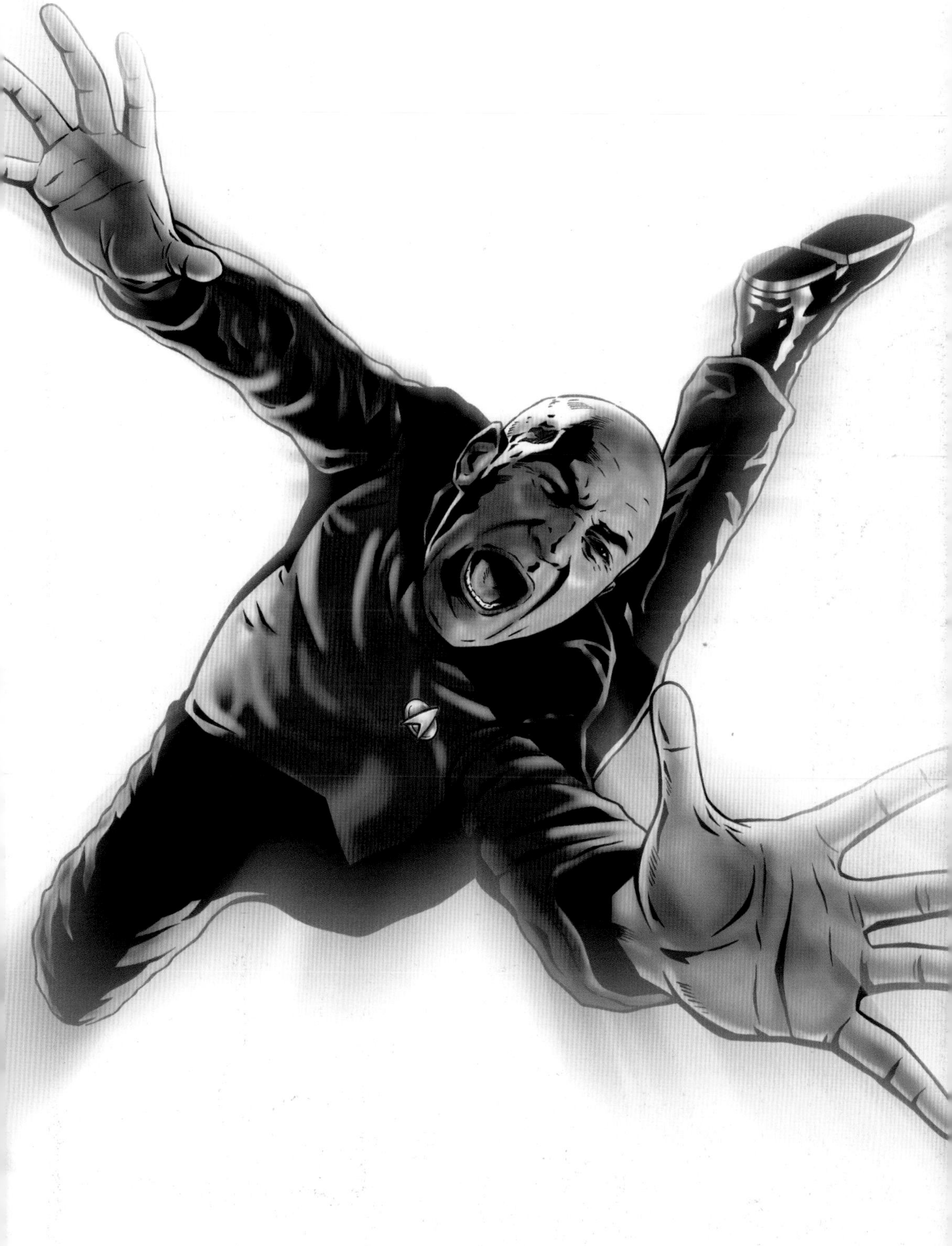

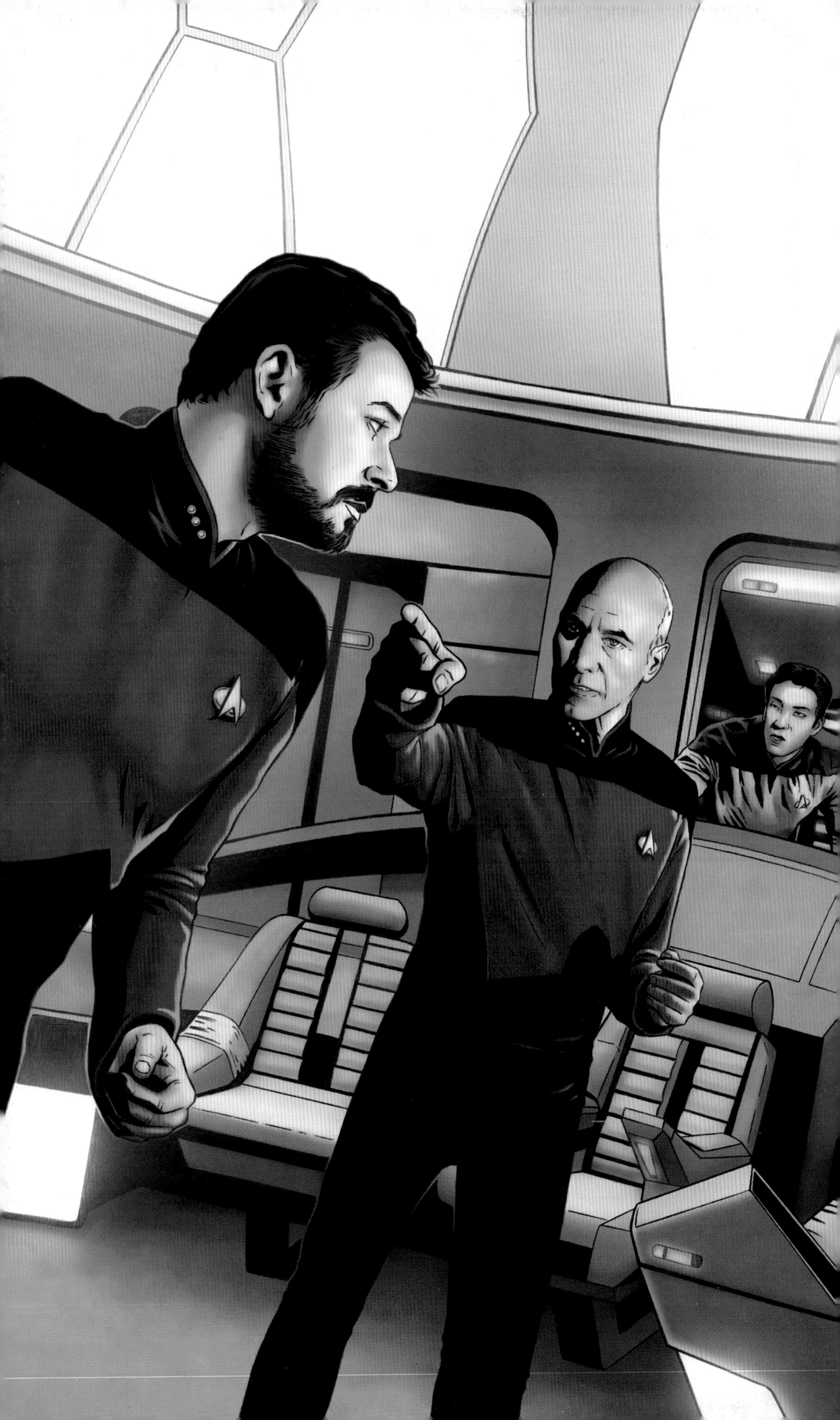

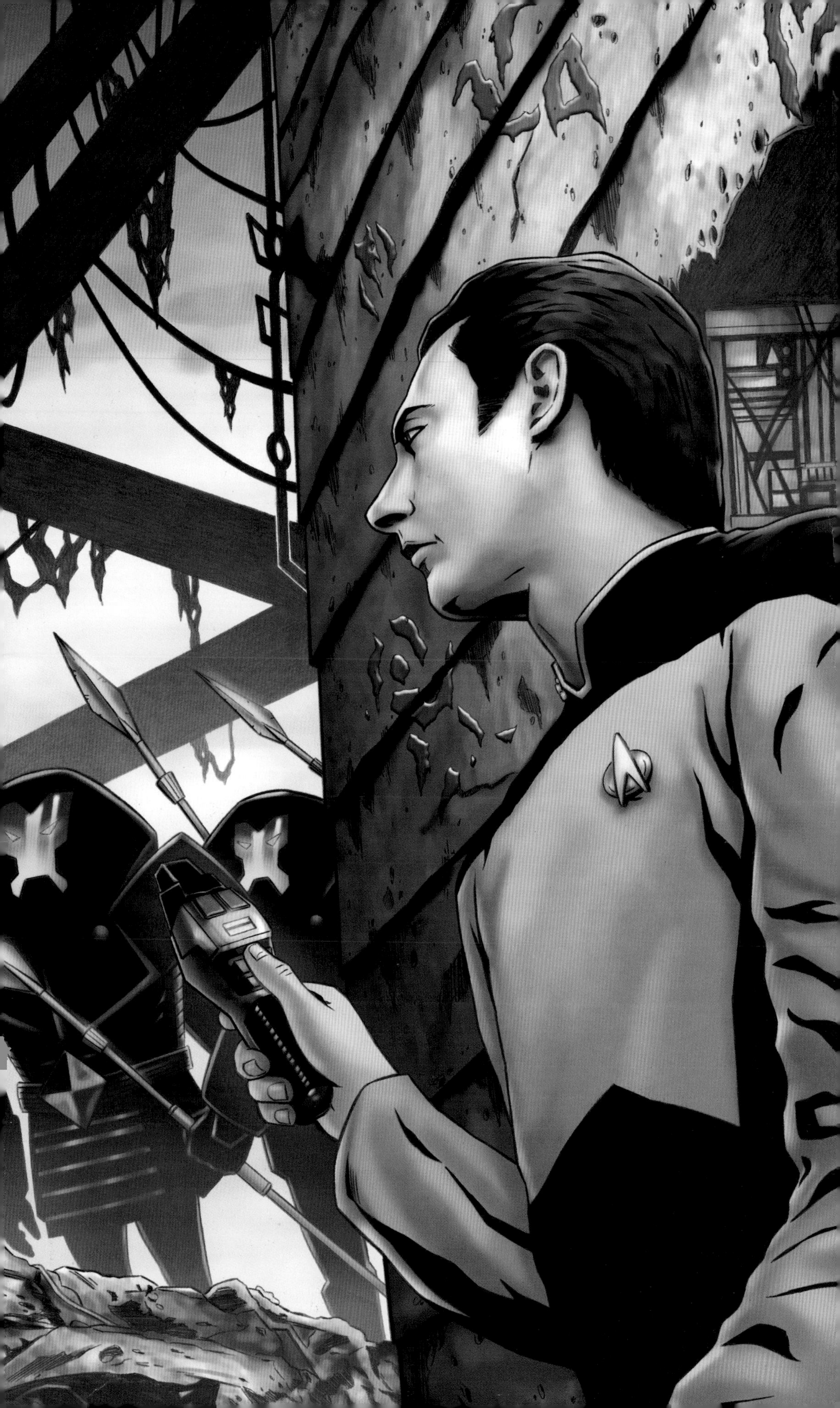

STAR TREK
THE NEXT GENERATION®
GHOSTS